BARBECUE
WHERE THERE'S SMOKE
THERE'S FLAVOUR

BARBECUE
WHERE THERE'S SMOKE
THERE'S FLAVOUR

Eric Treuille & Birgit Erath

Photography by
IAN O'LEARY

DK

A Dorling Kindersley Book

LONDON, NEW YORK, MUNICH
MELBOURNE, DELHI

EDITORIAL CONSULTANT
Rosie Kindersley

DESIGN AND ART DIRECTION
Stuart Jackman

PROJECT EDITOR
Julia Pemberton Hellums

EDITOR
Sally Somers

PRODUCTION CONTROLLER
Elizabeth Cherry

FOOD STYLING
Eric Treuille

First published in Great Britain in 2000
Reissued in Great Britain in 2007 and 2014
by Dorling Kindersley Limited
80 Strand London, WC2R 0RL

A Penguin Random House Company

1 3 5 7 9 8 6 4 2
001–255807–May/2014

Copyright © 2000 Dorling Kindersley Limited
Text copyright © Eric Treuille and Birgit Erath

All rights reserved. No part of this publication
may be reproduced, stored in a retrieval system,
or transmitted in any form or by any means,
electronic, mechanical, photocopying, recording
or otherwise, without prior written permission
of the copyright owner.

A CIP catalogue record for this book is
available from the British Library.

ISBN 978-1-4093-5271-6

Colour reproduction in Italy by GRB
Printed and bound by South China

discover more at
www.dk.com

CONTENTS

Introduction 6
Notes from the Cooks 7

THE GRILL
The Grill 8
The Tools 10
The Fire 12
The Food - Doneness 13

THE FLAVOURS
Flavours for the Grill 14
The Knowledge 16
The Spice - Salt, Pepper & Chillies 18
The Spice - Added Flavours 20
Mixes & Marinades 22
Marinating 26

THE RECIPES
Meat on the Grill 30
Seafood on the Grill 62
Chicken on the Grill 88
Vegetables on the Grill 116
Sauces & Salsas 130
Salads & Sides 144

THE MENUS 156
Notes from the Cooks on
Ingredients 158
Essential Skills 160
Index 162
Acknowledgements &
Mail Order Sources 167
How We Make
Our Books 168

INTRODUCTION

All around the world people cook over open fire. It's how cooking began and it has stood the test of time. It's today's favourite way to cook and it is easy to understand why. Grilling means no fuss, less fat, more flavour, most fun. Nothing brings out the best flavour in food quite like eating it sizzling hot off the barbecue grill.

Good food means a good time, and a gathering around the barbie makes any meal a celebration. Friends and family mix, mingle and unwind as steaks sear and ribs sizzle. Casual, yet a real occasion, a barbecue party sets appetites on fire.

There's something elemental about open-fire cooking. Could it be that those dancing flames, glowing embers and smoky aromas awaken our long-lost primordial selves?

Even people with the most hard-boiled "I can't cook" attitudes are unable to resist the excitement of cooking over coals.

We don't want to get too serious, because, to us, grilling isn't serious. This book is not a heavy-weight volume crammed with everything you need to know to grill like a pro. It's about having fun outdoors with food, flavour and fire.

Grilling shouldn't mean burnt steak, scorched chicken and other charred remains. Say goodbye to all that. Say hello to great grilled food every time. We've identified the key factors to guarantee grilling success, and we've made them simple.

To make our recipes, all you need are a few ingredients, hot coals and a sense of adventure. So relax. Just do it. Because we all love food hot off the grill. Come outside and join the party!

Eric Biquet

NOTES FROM THE COOKS

BEFORE YOU COOK read through the recipe carefully. Make sure you have all the equipment and ingredients required. In all recipes, vegetables are washed and peeled, unless otherwise stated.

ON PREHEATING

We have given instructions for indoor as well as outdoor grilling. But, whether grilling outdoors or indoors, be sure to allow enough time to get your grill up to the desired firepower. Successful grilling must sear the surface of food quickly to form a flavourful crust and to seal the succulent juices inside. Inadequate preheating means the crust does not form, the juices leak out, and you have uniformly tough, dry and tasteless results.

For charcoal barbecue grills, light up 30-40 minutes before you want to start grilling. This gives the coals time to reach the perfect temperature for a hot fire.

For gas barbecue grills, allow 10-15 minutes to preheat the lava rocks to the desired temperature.

For ridged cast iron grill pans, set over a medium high heat 3 minutes before grilling. To see if it is hot enough, splash a few drops of water on the surface: they should sizzle and evaporate immediately.

For overhead grills, allow 5-10 minutes to preheat an electric overhead grill and 3-5 minutes for a gas grill before you want to start.

ON TASTING

Always taste food as you cook and before you serve. Don't be afraid to add or change flavours to suit your palate - the fun of cooking is in experimenting, improvising, creating. Ingredients differ from day to day, season to season and kitchen to kitchen. Be prepared to adjust sweetness, sharpness, spiciness, and, most important of all, salt, to your own taste. The amount of salt and pepper used to season food makes the difference between good and great food.

SALT AND PEPPER

As a general guideline, allow 2 tsp salt and 1 tsp pepper for every 4 servings of meat. In practice, ingredients vary, palates vary and even salts vary, but this remains a good guideline.

ON MEASURING

Accurate measurements are essential if you want the same good results each time you follow a recipe. We have given measurements in metric and imperial in all the recipes. Always stick to one set of measurements. Never use a mixture of both in the same recipe.

Kitchen scales are the most accurate way to measure dry ingredients. We recommend using scales for all except the smallest amounts.

We recommend using cooks' measuring spoons when following a recipe. All spoon measurements in the book are level unless otherwise stated. To measure dry ingredients with a spoon, scoop the ingredient lightly from the storage container, then level the surface with the edge of a straight-bladed knife.

We use standard level spoon measurements:
- 1 tbsp - 15ml (½ floz)
- 1 tsp - 5ml (⅙ floz)

To measure liquids, choose a transparent glass or plastic measuring jug. Always place the jug on a flat surface and check for accuracy at eye level when pouring in a liquid to measure.

A final and important rule of measuring - never measure ingredients over the mixing bowl!

THE GRILL

THE BASIC EQUIPMENT

All you need is a fire, some food and a rack, so that the food doesn't actually end up in the fire. That's it. Anything from the latest, state-of-the-art model of barbecue grill to a simple set-up of a rack over a few stones on the beach will pretty much do the same job.

THE RULES FOR SAFETY AND SUCCESS

Get ahead. Our recipes are designed to let you know what steps can be done in advance. Follow our THINK AHEAD instructions, so that when it's time to get grilling, you're all set.

Get organized. Be sure to have everything you need to hand. Outdoor grilling is high speed, high heat cooking. Once the food hits the flames, there's no time to run back to the kitchen for tongs, salt, or platter.

Let it be. Food will always stick to the grill rack initially, but once a crisp crust has formed, it can be turned or moved with ease. Don't poke, prod or attempt to turn food during the first minute of cooking.

Don't overcrowd the grill rack. An overloaded barbecue grill means food will steam, not sear. You don't want to miss out on the crisply caramelised crust that makes great grilled food what it is.

Check frequently for doneness. Use our suggested cooking times as a guideline. Start checking a few minutes before the food is due to be done. Once food is overcooked, it is tough and dry, and there's no turning the clock back.

Don't wander off. On the safety front, you are, after all, playing with fire, and accidents can happen. On the culinary front, food cooks quickly over hot coals and deserting your post can mean the difference between chargrilled and downright charred.

Clean up. A clean grill rack stops food from sticking. A grill rack encrusted with burnt food will result in coals that flare up and new food that tastes of old food. Brush the grill rack with a stiff wire brush while it is still hot, to loosen any charred remains.

THE TOOLS

There are only a few accessories that we feel are really essential, with good-quality, long-handled tongs and a long metal spatula at the top of the list as must-haves for grilling.

1. Long-handled tongs
2. Long metal spatula
3. Hinged grill rack (round or square)
4. Flat metal skewers

5. Natural bristle basting brush
6. Bamboo skewers
7. Instant-read thermometer
8. Stiff wire brush for cleaning grill

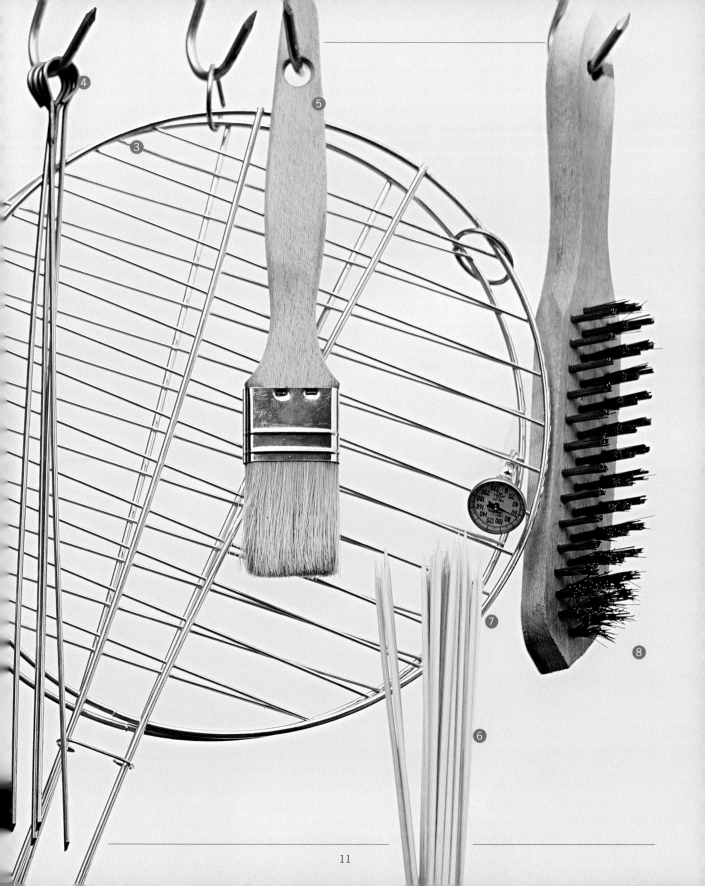

THE FIRE

Heat control is the key to successful grilling over charcoal. Building a good fire and judging its temperature are more crucial to success than the type or brand of barbecue grill you own or which sort of fuel you use.

HOW TO BUILD IT

How much charcoal you use depends on how much and what kind of food you intend to grill. The more food you are cooking, the longer your fire needs to burn hot.

Bear in mind that it's easier to reduce heat than to raise it, so, as a general rule, start out with more charcoal than you think you'll need.

Spread the charcoal in an even layer about 5cm (2in) deep and 5cm (2in) wider on all sides than the total surface area of the food you are going to grill.

HOW HOT?

The appropriate time to test the temperature of a fire is when the flames have died down. The coals should be glowing red and covered with a light dusting of fine grey ash.

For an approximate guide, hold the palm of your hand flat about 12.5cm (5in) above the coals and count in seconds.

If you can only keep your hand there for:
• 1-2 seconds - the coals are hot
• 3-4 seconds - the coals are medium hot
• 5-6 seconds - the coals are medium
• 6-7 seconds - the coals are medium low
• 8-9 seconds - the coals are low

HOW TO CONTROL IT

If the fire burns too hot, reduce the heat by spreading out the coals.

If the fire burns too low, boost the heat by pushing the coals closer together and adding more charcoal to the outer edges of the fire.

For a two-level fire with hotter and cooler areas, spread some of the hot coals out in a single layer, to create an area of slightly lower heat to one side of the barbecue. Use the hand test (see above) to check the difference in heat intensity. You can then grill ingredients requiring different cooking temperatures simultaneously.

THE FOOD - DONENESS

Exact grilling times are difficult to predict. Fires burn differently under different conditions. Various factors out of your control, including wind and temperature, make outdoor cooking an empirical, rather than an exact, science.

Use our suggested cooking times as a guideline. Watch the clock and check food a few minutes before it is due to be done. Never wait until food is on the plate; always check at the grill.

Experienced chefs and seasoned grill-meisters rely on the touch test (see below) for dense meat like beef, lamb and pork. We think it is also important to double-check for doneness with a knife.

When grilling more delicate things like fish and chicken, use the methods illustrated below. For grilled chicken on the bone, because of the health issues, we urge a policy of seeing is believing.

FORK TEST FOR FISH
Use a fork to prod the fish gently. It is done when the flesh is firm, just begining to flake and opaque through the centre but still moist.

TOUCH TEST FOR MEAT
The basic principle of the touch test is that meats become firmer as heat penetrates from the surface to the centre. Press the thickest part of the meat with your fingertip. The softer the meat is, the rarer it is. The firmer it is, the more well-done it is.

The touch test is a skill that can take some practice, but there is an easy shortcut for novice cooks. Press the meat with your finger. Compare the feel of the meat with the feel of the base of your thumb, as you move your thumb from fingertip to fingertip. The thumb muscle tenses and becomes progressively more resistant, corresponding to the different stages of doneness.

For rare, have your thumb touching your index finger (see above, top left).
For medium-rare, have your thumb touching your middle finger (see above, top right).
For medium, have your thumb touching your third finger (see above, bottom left).
For well-done, have your thumb touching your little finger (see above, bottom right).

KNIFE TEST FOR CHICKEN
Make a cut into the meat with a small, sharp knife. The flesh should be opaque throughout with no trace of pink at the bone.

FLAVOURS FOR THE GRILL

THE KNOWLEDGE

THE PRINCIPLES

From a simple drizzle of olive oil to a complex blend of aromatic spices, there's a world of different flavours to transform grilled food into a bigger and bolder taste experience. There are two main ways of flavouring grilled food: before food is grilled and after food is removed from the fire.

• Flavouring before grilling generally calls for immersing food in a marinade or flavour mix. This immersion can be as brief as a quick dip or as lengthy as an overnight soak.

• Flavouring after grilling focuses on adding an extra flavour dimension to food hot off the grill. Sauces and salsas (pages 130-143) can be served as a flavourful complement to just-grilled foods. Spice mixes (pages 22-25) can be sprinkled or drizzled over food hot off the grill.

• Marinades and flavour mixes are composed of three key elements: acids, oils and flavourings. These elements perform three distinct functions: to tenderize, moisten and flavour.

ACIDS: TENDERIZE AND ADD FLAVOUR

Citrus juices, vinegars and yoghurt are all acid ingredients that will boost the intensity of any marinade with a bright, sharp tang. Here are a few general tips:

• Use freshly squeezed citrus juices for maximum zing.

• Choose your vinegar according to the level of acid bite you want in your marinade.
• Balsamic vinegar is the most versatile of vinegars. A combination of sweet and sharp, it is ideal for a marinade or to drizzle lightly over food hot from the fire.
• Yoghurt is a uniquely all-purpose acid for marinating. It moistens as well as flavours and tenderizes.

OILS: PROVIDE MOISTURE

Lean, tender foods, such as fish and chicken, require the added moisture and protection provided by oil to combat the fierce heat of the fire. More resilient ingredients, such as beef and lamb, when marinated in acidic mixes, require oil to replace the moisture drawn out of the meat by the acid.

• Light, neutral oils, such as sunflower, contribute little flavour, but there are many other oils that have their own distinctive taste. Try using extra virgin olive oil or a nutty toasted sesame oil (see pages 20-21) for additional flavour.
• Oils can play their moisture-giving role at any stage of the grilling process: in marinades, as a baste during grilling, and as a flavour-packed mix to drizzle over grilled food just before serving.

ADDED FLAVOURS

Sweet flavourings take the sharp edge off an acidic marinade. Adding a bit of sugar to a flavour mix enhances the grilling process by helping to create a crispy caramelised crust on food exposed to the fire. Choose sweet flavourings that also add an extra dimension of flavour. We count fragrant honey, dark brown sugar and tangy pomegranate molasses (see pages 20 & 159) among our favourites.

Fresh flavourings add a fresh fragrance and depth to flavour mixes. Onions and garlic are pungent and vibrant. Asian flavours such as fresh ginger and lemon grass contribute a bright zing (see pages 20-21).

Fresh herbs should be chosen with care for the grill. Woody, robust herbs, such as oregano, rosemary and thyme, stand up to the strong flavour of food roasted over an open fire. Prolonged cooking over fierce heat eliminates the fragrant perfume of delicate herbs. Reserve them for making stuffings and for quickly grilled foods only.

Dried herbs are ideal flavour mixes for the grill (see pages 20-21). They contain aromatic oils that burst back into life when combined with the moisture of oil and the heat of the fire. Renew your supply of dried herbs regularly. On the grill, stale dried herbs will taste burnt and musty.

SALT AND PEPPER

Salt and pepper are extremely important flavourings for all grilled foods. Salt, however, draws out moisture, and with the moisture, flavour, from uncooked food, so always add salt after grilling. For maximum flavour, pepper should be freshly ground or cracked (see page 19). A good pepper grinder is an essential item for all cooks who value real flavour.

• Our preference is always for sea salt, fine or flaked (see page 19).

• Soy sauce (both Chinese and Japanese), fish sauce and miso are the salts of Asia (see page 19). When using, you should not require additional salt.

CHILLIES

Don't be afraid of chillies - the capsicum family offers much more than just the addition of fiery heat. With so many different varieties available in so many different forms, barbecue cooks have a fabulous range of flavours at their fingertips.

• Look out for "pure" chilli powders ground from one variety of chilli (see page 18). No kitchen cupboard is complete without crushed chilli flakes, Tabasco and Thai sweet chilli sauce (see pages 19 & 158).

THE SPICE
SALT, PEPPER & CHILLIES

Discerning use of seasoning makes the difference between good and great food. Professional chefs constantly taste their food for levels of salt and heat. The quality of salt matters, as different salts have different flavours and different levels of saltiness. We prefer sea salt, fine or flaked.

Nothing compares with the flavour of freshly ground pepper. A pepper grinder is an essential kitchen tool for any cook. Chillies come in many varieties and forms. Whether fresh, dry or bottled, chillies will contribute flavour and aroma as well as peppery heat.

1 Crushed chilli flakes
2 Ancho chilli powder
3 Kashmiri chilli powder
4 Scotch bonnets
5 Fresh red and green chillies
6 Chipotle peppers in adobo
7 Chinese hot chilli sauce
8 Thai sweet chilli sauce
9 Tabasco sauce
10 Thai fish sauce
11 Soy sauce
12 Coarse sea salt
13 Fine sea salt
14 Peppercorns
15 Freshly ground pepper

THE SPICE
ADDED FLAVOURS

Dedicated barbecue cooks should boast an international array of flavourings, condiments and sauces in their kitchen store-cupboard. Here are a few of our favourite flavourings from the global pantry.

1 Herbes de Provence
2 Greek oregano
3 Mexican oregano
4 Pomegranate molasses
5 Toasted sesame oil
6 Hoisin sauce
7 Rice wine vinegar
8 Citrus fruits
9 Red wine vinegar
10 Balsamic vinegar
11 Olive oil
12 Onions
13 Garlic
14 Smoked paprika
15 Hungarian paprika
16 Annatto
17 Tamarind
18 Miso
19 Wasabi
20 Fresh ginger

21 Pickled ginger
22 Lemon grass

21

CAROLINA HONEY GLAZE

MAKES 125ml (4floz)

2 tsp cajun seasoning
2 tbsp creamy dijon mustard
4 tbsp runny honey
2 tbsp cider vinegar or orange juice

Combine seasoning, mustard, honey and vinegar or juice. Use to marinate pork ribs up to 1 day in advance of grilling, pork chops up to 4 hours in advance, chicken wings up to 8 hours in advance and chicken breasts up to 4 hours in advance. Brush on more during grilling.

THINK AHEAD
Make up to 1 month in advance. Cover and refrigerate.

CAJUN SEASONING

MAKES 125ml (4floz)

2 tbsp white peppercorns
2 tbsp black peppercorns
2 tbsp cayenne pepper
1 tbsp garlic powder
1 tbsp onion powder
2 tsp dried thyme
1 tsp dried mustard powder
½ tsp ground fennel
½ tsp dried oregano
¼ tsp ground cumin

Grind ingredients together (see page 161). Use 1 tbsp for 4 servings of meat. Rub steak up to 6 hours in advance of grilling, pork ribs up to 1 day in advance, prawns up to 2 hours in advance, fish up to 30 minutes in advance and chicken breasts up to 6 hours in advance.

THINK AHEAD
Make up to 3 months in advance. Store in an airtight container at room temperature.

CAJUN SEASONING

ACHIOTE SEASONING

CAROLINA HONEY GLAZE

ACHIOTE SEASONING

MAKES 125ml (4floz)

3 tbsp annatto seeds
2 tbsp dried oregano
2 tbsp cumin seeds
1 tbsp coriander seeds
1 tbsp black peppercorns
6 cloves
1 tbsp ground allspice
½ tbsp ground cinnamon

Grind the annatto seeds in a spice grinder until reduced to a powder. Toast oregano, cumin, coriander, peppercorns and cloves (see page 161). Leave to cool. Add toasted spices to crushed annatto and grind together to form a powder.
Use 2 tbsp per 4 servings of meat. Rub on to pork chops up to 4 hours in advance of grilling, prawns up to 2 hours in advance, fish up to 30 minutes in advance and chicken wings up to 8 hours in advance.

THINK AHEAD
Make up to 3 months in advance. Store in an airtight container at room temperature.

CHARMOULA

MAKES 150ml (5floz)

1 handful flat-leaf parsley
1 handful fresh coriander
4 garlic cloves, crushed
1 tsp paprika
1 tsp ground cumin
½ tsp ground coriander
¼ tsp cayenne pepper
2 tbsp lemon juice
2 tbsp olive oil

Place parsley, coriander, garlic, paprika, cumin, coriander, cayenne, lemon juice and oil in a food processor or blender; pulse to a paste. Use 1 recipe for 4 servings of meat. Use to marinate lamb up to 1 day in advance of grilling, chicken breasts up to 6 hours in advance, prawns up to 2 hours in advance and fish up to 30 minutes in advance.

THINK AHEAD
Make up to 3 days in advance. Cover and refrigerate.

RECADO ROJO

MAKES 125ml (4floz)

3 tbsp achiote seasoning
6 garlic cloves, crushed
3 tbsp orange or pineapple juice
2 tbsp red wine vinegar
1 tbsp olive oil
1 tbsp runny honey

Combine seasoning, garlic, juice, vinegar, oil and honey.
Use to marinate pork chops up to 8 hours in advance of grilling, chicken breasts up to 4 hours in advance, prawns up to 2 hours in advance and fish up to 30 minutes in advance.

THINK AHEAD
Make up to 1 day in advance. Cover and refrigerate.

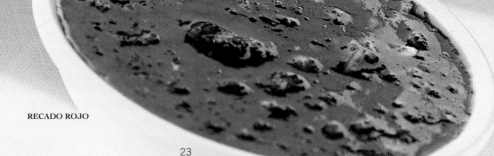

CHARMOULA

RECADO ROJO

SPICY JERK RUB

MAKES 125ml (4floz)

6 spring onions, chopped
2 scotch bonnet chillies or
 3 jalapeños, seeded and chopped
2 tbsp grated fresh ginger
4 garlic cloves, crushed
1 medium onion, chopped
1 tsp ground allspice
1 tsp dried thyme
¼ tsp cinnamon
¼ tsp grated nutmeg
2 tsp salt
1 tsp black pepper

1 tbsp rum
1 tbsp cider vinegar
1 tbsp sunflower oil

Place spring onions, chillies, ginger, garlic, onion, allspice, thyme, cinnamon, nutmeg, salt, pepper, rum, vinegar and oil in a food processor or blender; pulse to a paste. Use 1 recipe per 4 servings. Rub on to meat just before grilling.

THINK AHEAD
Make up to 1 day in advance. Cover and refrigerate.

JAMAICAN JERK SEASONING

MAKES 125ml (4floz)

2 tbsp onion powder
1 tbsp dried chives
1 tbsp dried thyme
1 tbsp ground allspice
1 tbsp salt
1 tbsp dark brown sugar
2 tsp black pepper
2 tsp cayenne pepper
2 tsp garlic powder
½ tsp grated nutmeg
½ tsp ground cinnamon

Combine onion powder, chives, thyme, allspice, salt, sugar, black pepper, cayenne pepper, garlic powder, nutmeg and cinnamon. Use 2 tbsp per 4 servings. Rub on to pork chops up to 4 hours in advance of grilling and chicken wings up to 8 hours in advance

THINK AHEAD
Make up to 3 months in advance. Store in an airtight container at room temperature.

SPICY JERK RUB

GARAM MASALA

JAMAICAN JERK SEASONING

GARAM MASALA

MAKES 125ml (4floz)

3 tbsp cardamom pods
2½ tbsp cumin seeds
2 tbsp coriander seeds
1½ tbsp black peppercorns
1 tbsp cloves
2 tsp ground cinnamon
1 tsp grated nutmeg

Lightly crush cardamom pods. Discard skins and reserve seeds. Toast cardamom seeds, cumin, coriander, peppercorns and cloves (see page 161). Leave to cool. Crush toasted spices to a powder (see page 161). Blend with cinnamon and nutmeg. Use 2 tbsp per 4 servings. Rub on to pork chops up to 8 hours in advance of grilling, chicken breasts up to 4 hours in advance, prawns up to 2 hours in advance and fish up to 30 minutes in advance.

THINK AHEAD
Make up to 3 months in advance. Store in an airtight container at room temperature.

SPICY TANDOORI MIX

MAKES 3½ TBSP

2 tsp kashmiri or other red chilli powder
1 tbsp paprika
2 tbsp garam masala

Combine chilli powder, paprika and garam masala. Use 1 recipe per 4 servings. Rub on to lamb up to 1 day in advance of grilling, prawns up to 2 hours in advance, fish up to 30 minutes in advance and chicken breasts, wings and drumsticks up to 6 hours in advance.

JERKED HONEY RUM GLAZE

MAKES 125ml (4floz)

1 tsp jerk seasoning
4 tbsp runny honey
2 tsp dark rum

Combine seasoning, honey and rum. Brush on to meat just before and during grilling.

THINK AHEAD
Make up to 1 month in advance. Cover and refrigerate.

SPICY TANDOORI MIX

JERKED HONEY RUM GLAZE

MARINATING

Always cover food tightly while marinating.

• The more completely the food is coated with a marinade, the quicker the flavouring process.

• If marinating in a dish, press cling film directly on to the food in order to expel any air.

• A sealed zip lock or oven roasting plastic bag works very well to coat and seal food completely in a marinade.

Always use non-reactive containers for marinating.

• Choose glass, pyrex, ceramic, stainless steel and plastic.

• Never use aluminium, foil, cast-iron or copper.

Never marinate foods beyond the recommended time.

• The idea is to achieve taste without toughness.

• If you over-marinate, what you may gain in flavour, you'll sacrifice in texture, as some acidic marinades begin to break meat down if it is left too long in a mix.

Always shake excess flavour mixes off food before cooking.

• Oil that drips on to the coals causes flare-ups, and flare-ups give you burnt, not flame-kissed, food.

Never mix raw and cooked.

• Don't put grilled food back in the same dish that you used for marinating. Bacteria will still be in the raw juices left behind in the dish, so be sure to use a clean dish for cooked food.

1 Heavy plastic zip-lock bags
2 Glass bowl
3 Glass dish
4 Plastic tray
5 Basting brush

THE RECIPES

MEAT ON THE GRILL

BEEF ESSENTIALS

WHAT TO GRILL

Always choose beef that is liberally marbled with fat. We recommend buying steaks from the tenderloin, loin, sirloin or rump. Beef tastes best when cooked briefly and quickly over a high heat. This method yields succulent, juicy results.

GETTING IT READY

Well marbled beef needs only a light brush of oil before grilling. To prevent flare-ups, trim outer fat and shake off excess marinade before placing meat on the grill.

PUTTING IT ON

To achieve professional-looking, criss-cross markings on a steak, place it on the grill until grill markings are clearly visible across the underside of meat, about 1 minute. Rotate the steak through 60° (the angle between 12 and 2 o'clock) and leave to sear 1 minute more. Turn steak over and repeat on the opposite side.

TAKING IT OFF

Use your finger to touch test for doneness. The meat should feel soft, firm and juicy to the touch (see page 13).
When using a meat thermometer, beef should read for 65°C (150°F) for medium rare and 75°C (170°F) for well done.

RESTING

For juicy, tender beef, always allow meat to relax and juices to settle inside the meat before serving. Cover loosely with foil to keep warm and let stand for 5 minutes.

FINAL FLAVOURING

Salting beef before cooking draws out the flavourful juices and toughens the flesh. Always add seasoning at the last minute but be sure not to forget before serving.

CHARGRILLED SIRLOIN STEAK WITH GARLIC PARSLEY BUTTER

SERVES 4

4 - 250g (8oz) sirloin steaks, 2.5cm (1in) thick
1 tbsp melted butter
1 tsp black pepper
salt
4 - 1cm (½in) slices garlic parsley butter (see page 140)

Brush steaks with melted butter. Sprinkle with pepper. Grill according to instructions below. Sprinkle with salt and leave to rest for 5 minutes. Serve warm, topped with garlic parsley butter.

OUTDOOR
Grill over hot coals for 3 minutes per side for rare, 4 minutes per side for medium rare, 6 minutes per side for well done.

INDOOR
Preheat a ridged cast iron grill pan over high heat. Grill for 3 minutes per side for rare, 4 minutes per side for medium rare, 6 minutes per side for well done.

COOKS' NOTE
Any of the flavoured butters on pages 140-141 - blue cheese, black olive or coriander chilli - would be delicious melted over this succulent steak.

CHARGRILLED T-BONE STEAK WITH CHIMI CHURRI SAUCE

SERVES 4

2 - 750g (1½lb) t-bone steaks, 2.5cm (1in) thick
1 tbsp olive oil
1 tsp black pepper
salt
1 recipe chimi churri sauce (see page 135)

Drizzle steaks with oil. Sprinkle with pepper. Grill according to instructions below.
Sprinkle with salt. Leave to rest for 5 minutes. To serve, cut around the bone to release
the meat. Cut the meat across into 5mm (¼in) slices. Serve hot with chimi churri sauce.

OUTDOOR
Grill over hot coals for 6 minutes per side for rare,
8 minutes per side for medium rare, 12 minutes per
side for well done.

INDOOR
Preheat a ridged cast iron grill pan over high heat. Grill
for 6 minutes per side for rare, 8 minutes per side for
medium rare, 12 minutes per side for well done.

CHARGRILLED FILLET STEAK WITH SALSA VERDE

SERVES 4

4 - 175g (6oz) fillet steaks, 5cm (2in) thick
1 tbsp olive oil
1 tsp black pepper
salt
1 recipe salsa verde (see page 134)

ESSENTIAL EQUIPMENT
kitchen string

Tie a piece of string around the middle of each steak to ensure a neat shape and even cooking. Rub steaks with oil and pepper. Grill according to instructions below. Sprinkle with salt and leave to rest for 5 minutes. Cut string and remove. Serve warm, topped with salsa verde.

OUTDOOR
Grill over hot coals for 3 minutes per side for rare, 4 minutes per side for medium rare, 6 minutes per side for well done.

INDOOR
Preheat a ridged cast iron grill pan over high heat. Grill for 3 minutes per side for rare, 4 minutes per side for medium rare, 6 minutes per side for well done.

SESAME SOY SKEWERED STEAKS

SERVES 4

**8 - 60g (2oz) fillet steaks,
  2.5cm (1in) thick**
4 spring onions

2 tbsp fresh grated ginger
3 garlic cloves, crushed
1 tsp crushed chilli flakes
½ tsp black pepper
1 tbsp sesame oil
2 tsp dark brown sugar
6 tbsp soy sauce
**1 tbsp rice vinegar or medium dry
  sherry**
1 tbsp sesame seeds

ESSENTIAL EQUIPMENT
8 – 25cm (10in) presoaked bamboo skewers

Place 2 steaks side by side on a tray.
Push one skewer diagonally through
both steaks. Push a second skewer
diagonally, in the opposite direction to
the first skewer, to secure the 2 steaks
together, forming a cross with the 2
skewers. Thread the end of a spring
onion on to the pointed end of one
skewer. Thread the other end of the
spring onion on to the pointed end of the
second skewer. Repeat with remaining
steaks, skewers and spring onions.
Combine ginger, garlic, chilli flakes,
pepper, oil, sugar, soy sauce, vinegar or
sherry and sesame seeds in a bowl. Pour
mixture over skewered steaks. Cover
and refrigerate for 30 minutes. Grill
according to instructions below.
Serve hot.

OUTDOOR
Grill over medium-hot
coals for 3 minutes per
side for rare, 4 minutes
per side for medium-
rare, 6 minutes per side
for well done.

INDOOR
Preheat overhead grill.
Grill for 3 minutes per
side for rare, 4 minutes
per side for medium-
rare, 6 minutes per side
for well done.

THINK AHEAD
Skewer and marinate steaks up to 8 hours in
advance. Cover and refrigerate.

SPICED BEEF FAJITAS WITH SALSA FRESCA AND GUACAMOLE

SERVES 4

FOR MARINADE
2 garlic cloves, crushed
½ tsp crushed chilli flakes
½ tsp ground cumin
½ tsp dried oregano
¼ tsp ground allspice
2 tbsp Mexican beer, or lager
1 tbsp olive oil

500g (1lb) rump steak, cut 2.5cm
  (1in) thick

FOR GUACAMOLE
2 fresh green chillies, seeded and
  finely chopped
2 tbsp finely chopped fresh coriander
4 tbsp lime juice
2 medium avocados, chopped
salt, black pepper

4 flour tortillas
salt, black pepper
1 handful shredded lettuce
1 recipe salsa fresca (see page 133)
125ml (4floz) sour cream

OUTDOOR
Grill over hot coals for 5 minutes per side for rare, 7 minutes per side for medium rare, 10 minutes per side for well done. Warm tortillas by setting directly over grill for 30 seconds each side.

INDOOR
Preheat a ridged cast iron grill pan over high heat. Grill for 5 minutes per side for rare, 7 minutes per side for medium rare, 10 minutes per side for well done. Warm tortillas by placing in grill pan for 30 seconds each side.

THINK AHEAD
Marinate beef up to 1 day in advance. Cover and refrigerate. Make guacamole up to 1 day in advance. Cover tightly with cling film, pressing directly on the guacamole to prevent contact with air, and refrigerate.

COOKS' NOTE
Fajitas are a classic of Tex-Mex cuisine. Skirt steak is the traditional cut to use. It is well worth asking your butcher for this lean, flat, intensely flavourful steak. Grill as directed for a truly authentic Tex-Mex fajita.

For marinade, combine garlic, chilli flakes, cumin, oregano, allspice, beer and oil. Add steak and turn to coat. Cover and refrigerate for 1 hour. For guacamole, combine chillies, coriander, lime juice and avocado. Mash with a potato masher until well combined but still chunky. Add salt and pepper to taste. Cover and refrigerate. Grill steak according to instructions opposite. Leave to stand for 5 minutes before carving on the diagonal into 1cm (½in) thick slices. Warm tortillas according to instructions opposite. Place steak slices on warmed tortillas. Sprinkle with salt and pepper. Top with lettuce, salsa fresca, guacamole and sour cream. Roll up and serve hot.

HUNGARIAN SPICED BEEF SKEWERS WITH SOUR CREAM

SERVES 4

500g (1lb) minced chuck steak
1 onion, grated
4 garlic cloves, crushed
2 tsp paprika
1 tsp dried marjoram
1 tsp ground caraway
1 tsp black pepper
2 tsp salt
salt and black pepper to sprinkle
150ml (5floz) sour cream to serve
1 recipe chargrilled garlic potato
  slices (see page 120), optional

ESSENTIAL EQUIPMENT
8 – 25cm (10in) presoaked bamboo skewers

Place minced steak, onion, garlic, paprika, marjoram, caraway, pepper and salt in a food processor; pulse until combined. Divide into 8 equal-sized portions. With wet hands, mould each portion round a separate skewer, shaping it into a sausage, about 20cm (8in) long. Grill according to instructions below. Sprinkle with salt and pepper. Serve hot with sour cream and chargrilled garlic potato slices, optional.

OUTDOOR
Grill over medium-hot coals, turning every 2 minutes, until well browned but still juicy and slightly pink inside, 8-10 minutes.

INDOOR
Preheat overhead grill. Grill, turning every 2 minutes, until well browned but still juicy and slightly pink inside, 8-10 minutes.

THINK AHEAD
Prepare and skewer satays up to 1 day in advance. Cover with cling film and refrigerate.

COOKS' NOTE
If you can find it, use Hungarian paprika, which is superior to the more widely available Spanish paprika. It has a sweet, sun-dried flavour and a bright colour.

CORIANDER BEEF SATAYS WITH HONEY TAMARIND GLAZE

SERVES 4

500g (1lb) minced chuck
  steak
2 tbsp grated fresh ginger
2 garlic cloves, crushed
1 onion, grated
1 handful fresh coriander
  leaves

1 tsp ground coriander
1 tsp ground turmeric
1 tsp chilli powder
½ tsp ground cumin
½ tsp ground cardamom
2 tsp salt
½ tsp black pepper

FOR GLAZE

1 tbsp grated fresh ginger
1 garlic clove, crushed
1½ tbsp tamarind paste
1½ tbsp runny honey

salt, black pepper

ESSENTIAL EQUIPMENT
8 – 35cm (14in) flat metal skewers

Place minced steak, ginger, garlic, onion, fresh coriander, ground coriander, turmeric, chilli powder, cumin, cardamom, salt and pepper in a food processor; pulse until combined. Divide into 8 equal-sized portions. With wet hands, mould each portion round a separate skewer, shaping it into a sausage, about 20cm (8in) long.

For glaze, combine ginger, garlic, tamarind and honey. Grill according to instructions below. Sprinkle with salt and pepper. Serve hot.

OUTDOOR
Grill over medium-hot coals, brushing with glaze, turning every 2 minutes, until well browned but still juicy and slightly pink inside, 8-10 minutes.

INDOOR
Preheat overhead grill. Brush with glaze and grill, turning every 2 minutes, until well browned but still juicy and slightly pink inside, 8-10 minutes.

THINK AHEAD
Prepare and skewer satays and make glaze up to 1 day in advance. Cover each with cling film and refrigerate.

COOKS' NOTE
Dark, shiny tamarind paste - sometimes referred to as concentrate - has a refreshing, sharp citrus flavour. It is usually available from Asian and Middle-Eastern stores. If you can't find it, use tamarind pulp. For this recipe, dissolve 1 tbsp pulp in 1 tbsp boiling water, then cool and sieve before using.

BEST BURGER WITH BLUE CHEESE BUTTER

SERVES 4

500g (1lb) minced chuck steak
2 tsp salt
1 tsp black pepper

4 - 1cm (½in) slices blue cheese
butter (see page 140)
4 sesame hamburger rolls, halved

Combine minced steak with salt and pepper. Divide into 4 equal-sized pieces and gently shape into 4 burgers about 2.5cm (1in) thick. Grill burgers and warm rolls according to instructions below. Top with butter and serve hot in sesame rolls.

OUTDOOR
Grill over hot coals for 3 minutes per side for rare, 4 minutes per side for medium rare, 5 minutes per side for well done. Place rolls cut side down on grill until warm and lightly golden, 1 minute.

INDOOR
Preheat a ridged cast iron grill pan over high heat. Grill for 3 minutes per side for rare, 4 minutes per side for medium rare, 5 minutes per side for well done. Place rolls cut side down on grill pan until warm and lightly golden, 1 minute.

THINK AHEAD
Shape burgers up to 1 day in advance. Cover with cling film and refrigerate.

COOKS' NOTE
Over-handling the meat when shaping will result in a tough, dry burger. To guarantee a juicy burger, handle the meat as little as possible.

BEST BURGER VARIATIONS
HERBED BURGER

Add 2 tsp fresh thyme leaves or 1 tsp dried thyme, 1 crushed garlic clove and 1 tbsp finely chopped onion to the minced steak. Serve with garlic parsley butter (see page 140) in place of blue cheese butter.

SPICY BURGER

Add ½ tsp tabasco, 1 tbsp worcestershire sauce and 1 tsp creamy dijon mustard to the minced steak. Serve with coriander chilli butter (see page 140) in place of blue cheese butter.

PORK ESSENTIALS

WHAT TO GRILL

Small, lean and tender cuts, such as chops and ribs, will stay moist during cooking if they are marinated before and basted well during grilling. Larger cuts need to be cut into strips or cubes, and skewered. It is important for pork to be completely cooked through. Sausages are ideal for the grill, as there is plenty of evenly distributed fat to keep the meat moist while cooking.

GETTING IT READY

Trim off excess fat to avoid flare-ups. Unlike lamb and beef, the fat surrounds pork meat rather than marbling it, so to achieve meat which is cooked through but still juicy, pork should be marinated or brushed with oil before going on the grill.

TAKING IT OFF

Pork should be cooked until the internal temperature reaches 65°C (150°F). The meat should be opaque throughout but still moist.

RESTING

For juicy, tender pork, always allow meat to relax and juices to settle inside the meat before serving. Cover loosely with foil to keep warm, and let stand for 5 minutes.

FINAL FLAVOURING

Salting pork before cooking draws out the flavourful juices and toughens the flesh. Always add seasoning at the last minute, but be sure not to forget.

MEXICAN SPICED PORK CHOPS WITH PINEAPPLE LIME SALSA

SERVES 4

4 pork chops, 2.5cm (1in) thick
4 garlic cloves, crushed
1 tsp dried oregano
1 tsp ground cumin
½ tsp ground coriander
½ tsp black pepper
¼ tsp ground cinnamon

2 tbsp red wine vinegar
3 tbsp orange juice
1 tbsp runny honey
1 tbsp olive oil
salt, black pepper
1 recipe pineapple lime salsa
   (see page 134)

Trim off excess fat from the chops. With scissors, cut snips through the remaining fat at 4cm (1½in) intervals. Combine garlic, oregano, cumin, coriander, black pepper, cinnamon, vinegar, orange juice, honey and oil. Pour mixture over chops, turning several times to coat thoroughly. Cover and refrigerate for 4 hours. Grill according to instructions below. Sprinkle with salt and pepper. Serve hot with pineapple lime salsa.

OUTDOOR
Grill over medium-hot coals until there is no trace of pink near the bone but the pork is still juicy, 8-10 minutes per side.

INDOOR
Preheat a ridged cast iron grill pan over high heat. Grill until there is no trace of pink near the bone but the pork is still juicy, 8–10 minutes per side.

THINK AHEAD
Marinate pork up to 1 day in advance. Cover and refrigerate.

BALSAMIC PEPPERED PORK CHOPS

SERVES 4

4 pork chops, 2.5cm (1in) thick
4 garlic cloves
2 tbsp whole black peppercorns
1 tbsp dried thyme
¼ tsp crushed chilli flakes
1 tbsp balsamic vinegar
3 tbsp olive oil
extra balsamic for basting

Trim off excess fat from the chop. With scissors, cut snips through the remaining fat at 4cm (1½in) intervals. Place garlic, peppercorns, thyme, chilli flakes, vinegar and oil in a food processor or blender; pulse to a coarse paste. Rub the paste over both sides of the chops. Grill according to instructions below. Serve hot.

OUTDOOR
Grill over medium-hot coals, basting with the extra balsamic vinegar, until there is no trace of pink near the bone but the pork is still juicy, 8-10 minutes per side.

INDOOR
Preheat a ridged cast iron grill pan over high heat. Grill, basting with the extra balsamic vinegar, until there is no trace of pink near the bone but the pork is still juicy, 8-10 minutes per side.

THINK AHEAD
Rub pork with paste up to 2 hours in advance. Cover and refrigerate.

COOKS' NOTE
Snipping the outer fat with scissors prevents the chops from curling and shrinking during cooking, allowing them to remain flat and to cook evenly.

ROSEMARY PEPPERED PORK CHOPS

SERVES 4

4 pork chops, 2.5cm (1in) thick
4 garlic cloves
2 tbsp whole black peppercorns
3 tbsp fresh rosemary leaves
  or 1 tbsp dried rosemary
1 tsp fennel seeds
¼ tsp crushed chilli flakes
1 tbsp lemon juice
3 tbsp olive oil
lemon wedges

Trim off excess fat from the chop. With scissors, cut snips through the remaining fat at 4cm (1½in) intervals. Place garlic, peppercorns, rosemary, fennel seeds, chilli flakes, lemon juice and oil in a food processor or blender; pulse to a coarse paste. Rub the paste over both sides of the chops. Grill according to instructions below. Sprinkle with salt. Serve hot with lemon wedges.

OUTDOOR
Grill over medium-hot coals until there is no trace of pink near the bone but the pork is still juicy, 8-10 minutes per side.

INDOOR
Preheat a ridged cast iron grill pan over high heat. Grill until there is no trace of pink near the bone but the pork is still juicy, 8-10 minutes per side.

THINK AHEAD
Rub pork with paste up to 2 hours in advance. Cover and refrigerate.

COOKS' NOTE
Snipping the outer fat with scissors prevents the chops from curling and shrinking during cooking, allowing them to remain flat and to cook evenly.

SWEET SOY GLAZED PORK

SERVES 4

500g (1lb) pork fillet, sliced and skewered (see opposite)
6 tbsp soy sauce
3 tbsp tomato ketchup

4 tbsp hoisin sauce
3 tbsp medium dry sherry
3 tbsp runny honey
3 tbsp dark brown sugar

ESSENTIAL EQUIPMENT
3 – 35cm (14in) flat metal skewers

Combine soy sauce, ketchup, hoisin, sherry, honey and sugar. Set aside 6 tbsp of the mixture. Spread remaining mixture over both sides of the pork skewers. Grill according to instructions below. Serve hot with the remaining mixture drizzled over.

OUTDOOR
Grill over medium-hot coals until pork is opaque but still juicy, 3 minutes per side.

INDOOR
Preheat overhead grill. Grill until pork is opaque but still juicy, 3 minutes per side.

THINK AHEAD
Marinate pork up to 4 hours in advance. Cover and refrigerate.

SLICING AND SKEWERING PORK FILLET
Slice the pork fillet against the grain of the meat into strips 0.5cm (¼in) thick and about 10-15cm (4-6in) long.

Lay the strips flat on a board, side by side. Thread on to 3 parallel skewers.

SPICY PORK SATAY

SERVES 4

500g (1lb) pork fillet,
sliced and skewered
  (see page 46)
2 lemon grass stalks
1 tbsp grated fresh ginger
2 garlic cloves, crushed
1 onion
2 tsp ground fennel

2 tsp ground cumin
2 tsp ground coriander
1 tsp turmeric
1 tbsp lime juice
1 tbsp sunflower oil
salt, black pepper
1 recipe spicy peanut sauce
  (see page 136) to serve

OUTDOOR
Grill over medium-hot coals until pork
is opaque but still juicy, 3 minutes
per side.

INDOOR
Preheat overhead grill. Grill until pork
is opaque but still juicy, 3 minutes
per side.

THINK AHEAD
Marinate pork up to 1 day in advance. Cover and refrigerate.

COOKS' NOTE
For maximum flavour, be sure to toast and crush all the spices freshly
(see page 161).

ESSENTIAL EQUIPMENT
12 – 25cm (10in) presoaked bamboo skewers

Remove and discard the tough outer skin from the lemon grass
stalks and roughly chop. Place lemon grass, ginger, garlic,
onion, fennel, cumin, coriander, turmeric, lime juice and oil
in a food processor or blender; pulse to form a smooth paste.
Spread paste over both sides of the pork skewers. Cover
and refrigerate for 4 hours. Grill according to instructions
opposite. Sprinkle with salt and pepper. Serve hot with spicy
peanut sauce.

GARLIC MUSTARD PORK SKEWERS

SERVES 4

2 garlic cloves, crushed
2 tbsp worcestershire sauce
2 tbsp soy sauce
4 tbsp tomato ketchup
1 tbsp tomato purée
1 tsp tabasco
2 tbsp cider vinegar
2 tsp paprika

2 tbsp grainy dijon
  mustard
2 tbsp creamy dijon
  mustard
4 tbsp runny honey
500g (1lb) pork fillet,
  sliced and skewered
  (see page 46)

ESSENTIAL EQUIPMENT
3 – 35cm (14in) flat metal skewers

Combine garlic, worcestershire sauce, soy sauce, tomato ketchup, tomato purée, tabasco, vinegar, paprika, mustards and honey. Set aside 6 tbsp of the glaze. Spread remaining glaze over both sides of the pork skewers. Grill according to instructions below. Serve hot with the remaining glaze.

OUTDOOR
Grill over medium-hot coals until pork is opaque but still juicy, 3 minutes per side.

INDOOR
Preheat overhead grill. Grill until pork is opaque but still juicy, 3 minutes per side.

THINK AHEAD
Marinate pork up to 4 hours in advance. Cover and refrigerate.

COOKS' NOTE
If you can find it, use smoked paprika for this recipe. Smoked paprika is a speciality paprika from Spain. Unlike other paprikas, the peppers are not sun-dried, but oak-smoked, before being ground. This gives it a deep, rusty red colour and a distinctive smoky flavour. Smoked paprika is available from mail order and speciality stores (see page 167).

THAI SWEET & SOUR RIBS

SERVES 4

2kg (4lb) pork spareribs
1 red onion, finely chopped
2 garlic cloves, crushed
1 tbsp grated fresh ginger
1 tbsp sunflower oil
125ml (4floz) pineapple juice
2 tbsp fish sauce
4 tbsp tomato purée
4 tbsp lime juice
2 tbsp runny honey
6 tbsp Thai sweet chilli sauce

Separate ribs by slicing between the bones with a large knife or cleaver. Simmer separated ribs in a large pan of salted water until just tender, about 30 minutes. Drain. Rinse under cold running water and drain again. Leave to cool completely. Place onion, garlic, ginger and oil in a small pan. Stir fry over medium heat until softened, 5-10 minutes. Add pineapple juice, fish sauce, tomato purée, lime juice, honey and 2 tbsp sweet chilli sauce. Bring to the boil. Simmer gently until thick, 10 minutes. Leave to cool completely. Brush the sweet sour mixture over the ribs. Grill according to instructions below, basting with the remaining chilli sauce throughout. Serve hot.

OUTDOOR
Grill over medium-hot coals, turning frequently and basting, until brown and crusty, 15 minutes.

INDOOR
Preheat overhead grill. Grill, removing from under the grill every 5 minutes to baste, until brown and crusty, 15 minutes.

THINK AHEAD
Pre-cook the ribs up to 1 day in advance. Cool completely. Cover with cling film and refrigerate. Make glaze up to 1 day in advance. Cover and refrigerate.

COOKS' NOTE
Pre-cook the ribs in simmering water to remove the layer of outer fat. This not only prevents flare-ups during cooking, but allows the rib meat to stay tender and juicy inside and crispy on the outside.

RIB VARIATION
SPICED HOISIN RIBS

Omit all ingredients for the sweet sour mixture. Combine instead 8 tbsp hoisin sauce, ½ tsp Chinese five-spice, 4 crushed garlic cloves, 2 tbsp grated fresh ginger, 2 tbsp medium dry sherry, 4 tbsp soy sauce, 2 tbsp hot Chinese sauce and 8 tbsp dark brown sugar. Reserve 2 tbsp hoisin mixture for basting. Brush remaining mixture over ribs. Grill according to recipe above.

MAKING SAUSAGES

Run water through the casings to check for any holes or tears.

Gather casing up on to the nozzle until you reach the end of the casing.

Twist the top of the bag until the filling is visible in the nozzle, to clear any air pockets before you begin.

Gently squeeze the bag so that the casing fills evenly and forms a long sausage.

Prick all over with a toothpick to prevent the sausage from bursting during cooking.

COOKS' NOTE

Most butchers will sell you sausage casing if you give them some advance notice. The casing should come packed in salt.

TOULOUSE SAUSAGES

SERVES 4

500g (1lb) piece boneless streaky pork belly
2 tsp salt
1 tsp black pepper
100ml (3½ floz) cold water
1 metre (3ft) sausage casings

ESSENTIAL EQUIPMENT
Piping bag fitted with large plain nozzle, hinged grill rack or 2 flat metal skewers

Remove the rind from the pork and cut into 2.5cm (1in) cubes. Place pork cubes, salt, pepper and water in a food processor; pulse until the ground pork begins to form a ball.

Rinse the casings under cold running water and soak in a large bowl of cold water. This will remove excess salt and make the casings more pliable. Run water through casings to check for any holes or tears. Insert the nozzle into one end of the casing. Gather casing up on to the nozzle until you reach the other end of the casing. Fill the piping bag with sausagemeat. Twist the top of the bag until the filling is visible in the nozzle. Gently squeeze the top of the piping bag so that the casing fills evenly with the sausagemeat and forms a long sausage. Prick the finished sausage all over with a toothpick. See illustrations opposite for guidance.

For outdoor grilling, place the coiled sausage in a hinged grill rack, if using. Alternatively, and for indoor cooking, secure by pushing 2 skewers across each other through the coiled sausage. Grill according to instructions below. Serve hot.

OUTDOOR
Grill over medium-hot coals until browned and cooked through, 8-10 minutes per side.

INDOOR
Preheat overhead grill. Grill until browned and cooked through, 8-10 minutes per side.

THINK AHEAD
Make sausages up to 1 day in advance. Cover with cling film and refrigerate.

SAUSAGE VARIATIONS

GARLIC SAUSAGES

Add 60g (2oz) crushed garlic cloves to the food processor with the pork cubes, salt, pepper and water. Prepare and stuff casing according to recipe above.

SPICY SAUSAGES

Add 2 tsp paprika, 1 seeded and finely chopped fresh red chilli and 4 crushed garlic cloves in the food processor with the pork cubes, salt, pepper and water. Prepare and stuff casing according to recipe above.

LAMB ESSENTIALS

PERFECT MEAT FOR THE GRILL
Lamb is the original inspiration for the Mediterranean's great tradition of outdoor feasting. The meat is liberally and evenly marbled with fat, making it the ideal meat for the grill.

GETTING IT READY
Cut off excess fat to avoid flare-ups. Pull off the thin transparent membrane surrounding the meat and trim off any connective tissue.

PUTTING IT ON
Remove small cuts from the refrigerator 30 minutes, and large cuts 45 minutes, before grilling. To avoid flare-ups, shake off excess marinade before placing on the grill.

TAKING IT OFF
The surface of lamb cooks much faster than the interior, which results in a crisp, browned exterior with juicy meat inside. Use your finger to touch test for doneness. The meat should feel soft, firm and juicy to the touch (see page 13). When using a meat thermometer, lamb should read 65°C (150°F) for rare, and 75°C (170°F) for well done.

RESTING
For juicy, tender lamb, and in particular for large cuts, allow meat to relax and the juices to settle inside the meat before carving. Cover loosely with foil to keep warm and let stand for 10 minutes.

FINAL FLAVOURING
Salting lamb before cooking draws out the flavourful juices and toughens the flesh. Always add seasoning at the last minute, but be sure not to forget to add any before serving.

BONING AND HERB-SKEWERING CHOPS
Trim off excess fat from cutlets. Cut around the bone to release the meat.

Pull the flap round each chop to make a round shape. With a small, sharp knife make a slit through the chop, passing first through the flap. Push the sharp end of the rosemary sprig through the slit to secure.

THINK AHEAD
Bone and skewer chops up to 1 day in advance. Cover and refrigerate.

COOKS' NOTE
You can use a bamboo or metal skewer instead of a rosemary sprig.

ROSEMARY LAMB CHOPS WITH MUSTARD MINT DRESSING

SERVES 4

8 - 10cm (4in) rosemary sprigs
8 lamb loin chops, boned
 (see opposite)
1 garlic clove, crushed
2 tsp black pepper
1 tbsp balsamic vinegar
1 tbsp olive oil
salt

FOR DRESSING
1 tbsp creamy dijon mustard
2 tbsp finely chopped fresh mint
3 tbsp lemon juice
6 tbsp olive oil
salt, black pepper

For skewers, strip the leaves from the rosemary stalks, leaving a few leaves at one end of each stalk. Sharpen the other end to a point with a knife. Use sprigs to skewer lamb (see opposite). Combine garlic, pepper, vinegar and oil. Rub on to both sides of lamb. Cover and refrigerate for 30 minutes.

For dressing, combine mustard, mint and lemon juice. Gradually whisk in oil to make a thick dressing. Add salt and pepper to taste. Grill skewered lamb according to instructions below. Sprinkle with salt and pepper. Spoon over dressing and serve hot.

OUTDOOR
Grill over hot coals for 3 minutes per side for medium rare, 5 minutes per side for well done.

INDOOR
Preheat a ridged cast iron grill pan over high heat. Grill for 3 minutes per side for medium rare, 5 minutes per side for well done.

THINK AHEAD
Skewer and rub lamb up to 1 day in advance. Cover tightly with cling film and refrigerate. Make dressing up to 4 hours in advance. Cover and store at room temperature.

BUTTERFLIED LEG OF LAMB WITH ANCHOVY, PROSCIUTTO AND PARSLEY

SERVES 4 - 6

FOR PASTE
60g (2oz) prosciutto
6 anchovy fillets
1 handful flat-leaf parsley
2 garlic cloves
1 tbsp balsamic vinegar

2kg (4lb) leg of lamb, butterflied
  (see opposite)
2 tbsp balsamic vinegar for drizzling
salt, black pepper
1 recipe salsa verde (see page 134)

ESSENTIAL EQUIPMENT
2 - 35cm (14in) flat metal skewers

Place prosciutto, anchovies, parsley, garlic and vinegar in a food processor or blender; pulse to a smooth paste. Place lamb skin side down. With a sharp knife, cut 1cm (½in) deep slits across the lamb about 5cm (2in) apart. Push the paste deep into the slits. Insert skewers diagonally from opposite corners through butterflied lamb. Grill according to instructions below, drizzling balsamic vinegar on both sides during cooking. Remove to a board, cover with foil and leave to rest for 10 minutes before slicing. Sprinkle with salt and pepper. Serve warm with salsa verde, optional.

OUTDOOR
Grill over medium-hot coals, turning once, for 15 minutes per side for medium rare or 20 minutes per side for well done.

INDOOR
Preheat overhead grill. Arrange lamb on a wire rack over an oven tray. Grill, turning once, for 15 minutes per side for medium rare or 20 minutes per side for well done.

THINK AHEAD
Make paste up to 2 days in advance. Cover and refrigerate. Prepare lamb and stuff with paste up to 1 day in advance. Double wrap in cling film and refrigerate. Remove from refrigerator 45 minutes before grilling.

COOKS' NOTE
Skewering the butterflied lamb helps keep the meat together and also makes it easier to move on the grill.

BUTTERFLYING LEG OF LAMB
Put the leg of lamb on a board, skin side down. Cut round the exposed bone at the wide end of the leg. Cut the bone free at the joint and detach. Cut a slit along the length of the bone to expose and loosen. Use short, shallow cuts and scrape with the knife blade to release the meat from the bone. Remove bone.
Keeping the blade of the knife horizontal, make a lengthwise slit along the thick section of the meat next to the cavity left by the leg bone. Open out the flap and spread the meat flat like a book. Make another horizontal cut into the thick meat opposite and open out flat to form a "butterfly" shape with the entire piece.

COOKS' NOTE
Butterflying is a very useful technique for preparing meat for the grill. It allows the home chef to grill a large cut of meat in a quarter of time it would take to roast it. You'll find a boned joint easier to carve with less waste.

ROLLING BUTTERFLIED LEG OF LAMB
Spread the meat evenly with seasoning and herbs. Roll up lengthwise as tightly as possible. Place roll seam side down on a board.

Secure the roll with string. Starting in the centre, tie the meat tightly at 2cm (¾in) intervals.

Cut between the strings to make equal-sized steaks.

COOKS' NOTE
This technique transforms a leg of lamb into boneless individual portions that have all the flavour of the whole cut, but can be cooked and served with speed and ease.

LEG OF LAMB STEAKS WITH BLACK OLIVE BUTTER

SERVES 4

**2kg (4lb) leg of lamb, butterflied
  (see page 54)
1 tbsp salt
2 tsp black pepper**

**3 tbsp stripped fresh thyme leaves
1 recipe black olive butter
  (see page 140)**

ESSENTIAL EQUIPMENT
kitchen string

Sprinkle the meat evenly with salt, pepper and thyme. Roll up, secure with string and cut into steaks (see opposite). Grill according to instructions below. Just before removing from the grill, top each steak with a slice of black olive butter.

OUTDOOR
Grill over medium hot coals, turning once, 5 minutes per side for medium rare or 8 minutes per side for well done.

INDOOR
Preheat a ridged cast iron grill over high heat. Grill, turning once, 5 minutes per side for medium rare or 8 minutes per side for well done.

THINK AHEAD
Roll, stuff and slice lamb up to 2 days in advance. Double wrap in cling film and refrigerate. Remove to room temperature 20 minutes before grilling.

COOKS' NOTE
For a butter-free alternative, we suggest serving the lamb steaks with spiced chickpea sauce (see page 137) in place of the black olive butter.

BUTTERFLIED LEG OF LAMB PERSILLADE

2kg (4lb) leg of lamb, butterflied (see page 54)
1 tbsp salt
2 tsp black pepper
6 garlic cloves, sliced
2 handfuls flat-leaf parsley, roughly chopped

ESSENTIAL EQUIPMENT
3 - 35cm (14in) flat metal skewers

Prepare the butterflied lamb for stuffing by slicing it open again (see opposite). Sprinkle the meat evenly with salt and pepper. Spread garlic and parsley over one half of the meat (see opposite). Fold in half and secure with skewers (see opposite). Grill according to instructions below. Remove to a cutting board, cover with foil and leave to rest for 5 minutes before slicing.

OUTDOOR
Grill over medium hot coals, turning once, for 15 minutes per side for medium rare or 20 minutes per side for well done.

INDOOR
Preheat overhead grill. Arrange lamb on a wire rack over an oven tray. Grill, turning once, for 15 minutes per side for medium rare or 20 minutes per side for well done.

THINK AHEAD
Slice, stuff and skewer lamb up to 2 days in advance. Double wrap in cling film and refrigerate. Remove to room temperature 45 minutes before grilling.

COOKS' NOTE
Serve with potato focaccia with thyme (see page 155) or creamy potato salad with celery and chives (see page 148).

STUFFING BUTTERFLIED LEG OF LAMB
Hold the meat firmly with the flat of your hand. Keeping the blade of the knife horizontal, slice into the thickest part of the meat again to open an additional flap for stuffing.

Sprinkle over the stuffing.

Thread the skewers through both sides of the meat to secure.

COOKS' NOTE
Here we slice a butterflied leg in half again to make a pocket for flavourful stuffing. This makes spectacular presentation that never fails to impress.

CORIANDER LAMB PITTA WRAP

SERVES 4

500g (1lb) boneless lamb, cut into 4cm (1½in) cubes (see opposite)

FOR MARINADE
1½ tsp ground coriander
½ tsp ground cumin
¼ tsp ground allspice
¼ tsp ground cinnamon
2 tbsp lemon juice
2 tbsp olive oil
1 tomato, halved

½ medium onion
2 garlic cloves

FOR WRAP
4 pitta or flatbreads
1 handful shredded lettuce
4 tomatoes, cut into wedges
16 fresh mint leaves
1 recipe lemon tahini sauce (see page 132)
salt, black pepper

ESSENTIAL EQUIPMENT
4 – 35cm (14in) flat metal skewers

Place coriander, cumin, allspice, cinnamon, lemon juice, oil, tomato, onion and garlic in food processor or blender; pulse to form a thick paste. In a bowl, combine paste with lamb cubes, tossing to coat evenly. Cover and refrigerate for 2 hours. Thread lamb on to skewers. Grill according to instructions below. Split open and separate each pitta into 2 halves. Stack 2 pitta halves cut side up. Using a fork, slide the lamb pieces from 1 skewer on to the pitta. Top with a quarter of the lettuce, tomatoes and mint. Spoon over lemon tahini sauce. Sprinkle with salt and pepper and roll up. Repeat with remaining pitta, lamb, lettuce, tomatoes, mint and tahini sauce. Serve hot.

OUTDOOR
Grill over medium-hot coals, turning every 2 minutes, until well browned but still juicy and slightly pink inside, 8-10 minutes. Place pitta halves directly on the grill until just warm, about 30 seconds per side.

INDOOR
Preheat overhead grill. Grill, turning every 2 minutes, until well browned but still juicy and slightly pink inside, 8-10 minutes. Briefly warm pitta halves under the grill, about 15 seconds per side.

THINK AHEAD
Marinate lamb up to 1 day in advance. Cover and refrigerate.

BONING SHOULDER
Place shoulder skin side down. Cut a slit along the length of the two bones to expose. Cut and scrape the meat free from the shoulder bone. Cut through the joint to free the shoulder bone.

Cut through the meat on either side of the blade bone. Scraping the bone free, pull away the blade bone from the meat.

CUBING BONELESS SHOULDER
Trim off excess fat. Cut the meat into 4cm (1½in) strips.
Cut the strips into 4cm (1½in) cubes. You will need 20 cubes for 4 servings.

THINK AHEAD
Bone and cube lamb shoulder up to 2 days in advance. Cover tightly with cling film and refrigerate.

COOKS' NOTE
You need about 1kg (2lb) lamb shoulder on the bone to yield about 500g (1lb) boneless lamb. If you prefer a leaner cut, choose boneless leg of lamb.

LAMB TIKKA MASALA

SERVES 4

500g (1lb) boneless lamb, cut into 4cm (1½in) cubes
  (see page 58)
2 tbsp grated fresh ginger
4 garlic cloves, crushed
1 fresh green chilli, seeded and finely chopped
2 tbsp finely chopped fresh coriander
2 tbsp garam masala mix (see page 25)
1 tsp ground turmeric
2 tbsp red wine vinegar
150ml (5floz) Greek-style yoghurt
20 fresh bay leaves
20 fresh whole green chillies
salt, black pepper
4 naan or other flat bread
1 recipe cucumber yoghurt raita (see page 138), optional

ESSENTIAL EQUIPMENT
4 – 35cm (14in) flat metal skewers

Combine lamb cubes, ginger, garlic, chilli, fresh coriander,
masala mix, turmeric, vinegar and yoghurt. Toss well to coat
evenly. Cover and refrigerate for 2 hours. Thread lamb cubes,
bay leaves and chillies on to skewers. Grill lamb skewers and
warm naan according to instructions below. Sprinkle with salt
and pepper. Serve hot with warm naan and cucumber
yoghurt raita, optional.

OUTDOOR
Grill over medium-hot coals, turning
every 2 minutes, until well browned but
still juicy and slightly pink inside, 8-10
minutes. Warm the naan by setting
directly on the grill, 1 minute per side.

INDOOR
Preheat overhead grill. Grill, turning
every 2 minutes, until well browned
but still juicy and slightly pink inside,
8-10 minutes. Briefly warm the naan
under the grill, 30 seconds per side.

THINK AHEAD
Marinate lamb cubes up to 1 day in advance. Cover and refrigerate.

SPICED COCONUT LAMB SATAYS

SERVES 4

500g (1lb) boneless lamb, cut into 4cm (1½in) cubes
  (see page 58)
1 onion, chopped
2 garlic cloves, crushed
2 fresh red chillies, seeded and chopped
1 tbsp grated fresh ginger
1 tsp ground coriander
1 tbsp tamarind paste or lime juice
3 tbsp coconut milk
1 tbsp soy sauce
1 tbsp dark brown sugar
salt, black pepper
1 recipe spicy peanut sauce (see page 136), optional

ESSENTIAL EQUIPMENT
4 – 35cm (14in) flat metal skewers

Place onion, garlic, chillies, ginger, coriander, tamarind or lime
juice, coconut milk, soy sauce and sugar in food processor or
blender; pulse to form a paste. In a bowl, combine paste with
lamb cubes, tossing to coat evenly. Cover and refrigerate for
2 hours. Thread lamb on to skewers. Grill according to
instructions below. Sprinkle with salt and pepper. Serve hot
with spicy peanut sauce, optional.

OUTDOOR
Grill over medium-hot coals, turning
every 2 minutes, until well browned
but still juicy and slightly pink inside,
8-10 minutes.

INDOOR
Preheat overhead grill. Grill, turning
every 2 minutes, until well browned
but still juicy and slightly pink inside,
8-10 minutes.

THINK AHEAD
Marinate lamb up to 1 day in advance. Cover and refrigerate.

COOKS' NOTE
Dark, shiny tamarind paste - sometimes referred to as concentrate - has a
refreshing, sharp citrus flavour. It is usually found in Asian and Middle-Eastern stores.
If you can't find it, use tamarind pulp. For this recipe, dissolve 2 tbsp pulp in
4 tbsp boiling water, then cool and sieve before using. Alternatively, use lime juice.

HONEY HARISSA KOFTE

SERVES 4

500g (1lb) minced lamb
1 onion, grated
4 garlic cloves, crushed
2 tbsp finely chopped fresh mint
1 tbsp runny honey
1 tbsp tomato purée
3 tsp ground coriander
2 tsp ground cumin
1 tsp ground caraway seeds
1 tsp crushed chilli flakes
1½ tsp salt
½ tsp black pepper
1 recipe radish tzatziki (see page 135), optional

ESSENTIAL EQUIPMENT
8 – 25cm (10in) presoaked bamboo skewers

Place minced lamb, onion, garlic, mint, honey, tomato purée, coriander, cumin, caraway, chilli flakes, salt and pepper in a food processor; pulse until combined. Divide into 8 equal-sized portions. With wet hands, mould each portion round a separate skewer, shaping it into a sausage, about 15cm (6in) long. Grill according to instructions below. Sprinkle with salt and pepper. Serve hot with radish tzatziki, optional.

OUTDOOR
Grill over medium-hot coals, turning every 2 minutes, until well browned but still juicy and slightly pink inside, 8-10 minutes.

INDOOR
Preheat overhead grill. Grill, turning every 2 minutes, until well browned but still juicy and slightly pink inside, 8-10 minutes.

THINK AHEAD
Prepare and skewer kofte up to 1 day in advance. Cover with cling film and refrigerate.

CHARMOULA LAMB KOFTE

SERVES 4

500g (1lb) minced lamb
1 onion, grated
½ tsp black pepper
1½ tsp salt
1 recipe charmoula (see page 23)
1 recipe spiced chickpea sauce (see page 137), optional

ESSENTIAL EQUIPMENT
8 – 35cm (14in) flat metal skewers

Place lamb, onion, salt, black pepper and charmoula in a food processor; pulse until combined. Divide into 8 equal-sized portions. With wet hands, mould each portion round a separate skewer, shaping it into a sausage, about 15cm (6in) long. Grill according to instructions below. Sprinkle with salt and pepper. Serve hot with spiced chickpea sauce, optional.

OUTDOOR
Grill over medium-hot coals, turning every 2 minutes, until well browned but still juicy and slightly pink inside, 8-10 minutes.

INDOOR
Preheat overhead grill. Grill, turning every 2 minutes, until well browned but still juicy and slightly pink inside, 8-10 minutes.

THINK AHEAD
Prepare and skewer kofte up to 1 day in advance. Cover with cling film and refrigerate.

SKEWERING AND SLASHING FILLETS
Cut the neck fillets into four equal-sized pieces. Thread a skewer lengthwise through the middle of each piece.

With a sharp knife, make cuts approximately 2½cm (1in) apart down the length of each skewered piece.

THINK AHEAD
Skewer and slash fillets up to 1 day in advance. Cover and refrigerate.

COOKS' NOTE
Slashing lamb ensures that the marinade will penetrate the meat completely, and that the meat will cook evenly.

SKEWERED CUMIN LAMB WITH GARLIC YOGHURT SAUCE

SERVES 4

500g (1lb) boned lamb neck fillets, skewered and slashed (see opposite)
FOR MARINADE
2 garlic cloves, crushed
2 tbsp cumin seeds, toasted and roughly pounded (see page 161)
½ tsp ground coriander
½ tsp crushed chilli flakes
1 tbsp lemon juice
1 tbsp olive oil

FOR SAUCE
2 whole unpeeled garlic heads
1 tbsp olive oil
salt, black pepper
2 tsp creamy dijon mustard
2 tbsp balsamic vinegar
2 tbsp double cream
1 handful flat-leaf parsley
150ml (5floz) Greek-style yoghurt
salt, black pepper

ESSENTIAL EQUIPMENT
4 – 25cm (10in) presoaked bamboo skewers

For marinade, combine garlic, cumin, coriander, chilli flakes, lemon juice and oil. Rub over skewered lamb fillets. Cover and refrigerate for 1 hour. For sauce, preheat oven to 180°C (350°F) gas 4. Slice off top of both garlic heads, cutting through the tops of the cloves. Place cut-side up in oven tray. Drizzle over olive oil and sprinkle with salt and pepper. Roast until completely soft, 1 hour. Leave until cool enough to handle. Squeeze out cloves from papery skins into a food processor or blender. Add mustard, vinegar, cream, parsley and yoghurt; pulse until smooth. Add salt and pepper to taste. Grill lamb according to instructions below. Sprinkle lamb with salt and pepper. Serve hot with the garlic yoghurt sauce.

OUTDOOR
Grill over medium-hot coals, turning every 2 minutes, 8 minutes for medium rare, 12 minutes for well done.

INDOOR
Preheat a ridged cast iron grill pan over high heat. Grill, turning every 2 minutes, 8 minutes for medium rare, 12 minutes for well done.

THINK AHEAD
Make sauce up to 1 day in advance. Marinate lamb up to 1 day in advance. Cover and refrigerate.

COOKS' NOTE
Spiced chickpea sauce (see page 137) or radish tzatziki (see page 135) are excellent alternatives to the garlic yoghurt sauce served with this Middle-Eastern-spiced lamb dish.

SEAFOOD ON THE GRILL

PRAWNS WITH SALSA FRESCA

SERVES 4

1 recipe salsa fresca (see page 133)
375g (13oz) medium prawns, cooked
  and peeled
2 tbsp chopped fresh coriander

2 tbsp sour cream
salt, black pepper, tabasco
1 large bag plain, lightly salted
  tortilla chips

ESSENTIAL EQUIPMENT
heavy cast iron frying pan

Set dry pan over grill or stove as instructed below. When pan is hot, add salsa.
When salsa is bubbling add prawns and stir fry until prawns are hot, 1 minute.
Remove from heat. Stir in coriander and cream. Add salt, pepper and tabasco to
taste. Add a handful of tortilla chips. Serve hot, with extra tortilla chips and sour
cream for dipping.

OUTDOOR
On a charcoal grill, set pan over hot, flaming coals.

INDOOR
Set pan on stove over high heat.

SPICY MASALA PRAWNS

SERVES 4

4 tbsp garam masala mix
  (see page 25)
1 tsp chilli powder
2 tbsp paprika
2 tsp turmeric
1 tsp ground coriander
2 tsp salt
4 garlic cloves, crushed
1 tbsp grated fresh ginger
1 tbsp lemon juice
125g (4oz) butter, melted
20 raw unpeeled tiger prawns
lemon wedges

ESSENTIAL EQUIPMENT
20 - 25cm (10in) presoaked bamboo skewers

Combine garam masala mix, chilli
powder, paprika, turmeric, coriander,
salt, garlic, ginger, lemon juice and
butter to make a paste. Rub paste
thoroughly into prawns to coat evenly.
Skewer each prawn on to the end of
a single skewer. Cover with cling film
and refrigerate for 30 minutes. Grill
according to instructions below. Serve
with lemon wedges.

OUTDOOR
Grill over medium-hot
coals until the shell is
pink and the flesh is
opaque, 3 minutes
per side.

INDOOR
Preheat overhead grill.
Grill until the shell is
pink and the flesh
is opaque, 3 minutes
per side.

THINK AHEAD
Rub prawns with paste up to 2 hours in advance.
Cover and refrigerate.

COOKS' NOTE
Use Kashmiri chilli powder for an authentically Indian
flavour and colour. This chilli powder is made from
the mildly spicy and pungent chillies that are
traditionally used in tandoori dishes.

SWEET SESAME PRAWNS

SERVES 4

1 tbsp sesame seeds
1 tbsp sesame oil
2 garlic cloves, crushed
1 tbsp soy sauce
1 tbsp mirin
20 raw tiger prawns, peeled
lime wedges

ESSENTIAL EQUIPMENT
4 - 25cm (10in) presoaked bamboo skewers

Combine sesame seeds, sesame oil, garlic, soy sauce and mirin. Add prawns and toss to coat evenly. Thread 5 prawns on to each presoaked skewer. Repeat with remaining prawns and skewers. Cover with cling film and refrigerate for 30 minutes. Grill according to instructions below. Serve with lime wedges.

OUTDOOR
Grill over medium-hot coals until the shell is pink and the flesh is opaque, 3 minutes per side.

INDOOR
Preheat overhead grill. Grill until the shell is pink and the flesh is opaque, 3 minutes per side.

THINK AHEAD
Marinate prawns up to 2 hours in advance. Cover and refrigerate.

LEMON CHILLI PRAWNS

SERVES 4

3 tbsp lemon juice
½ tbsp Chinese hot chilli sauce
1 tbsp grated fresh ginger
2 garlic cloves, crushed

2 tbsp chopped fresh coriander
1 tbsp soy sauce
1 tbsp runny honey
20 raw unpeeled tiger prawns

ESSENTIAL EQUIPMENT
8 - 25cm (10in) presoaked bamboo skewers

Combine lemon juice, chilli sauce, ginger, garlic, coriander, soy sauce and honey. Add prawns and toss to coat evenly. Thread 5 prawns on to parallel skewers. Repeat with remaining prawns and skewers. Cover with cling film and refrigerate for 30 minutes. Grill according to instructions below.

OUTDOOR
Grill over medium-hot coals until the shell is pink and the flesh is opaque, 3 minutes per side.

INDOOR
Preheat overhead grill. Grill until the shell is pink and the flesh is opaque, 3 minutes per side.

THINK AHEAD
Marinate prawns up to 2 hours in advance. Cover and refrigerate.

PRAWNS WITH TAMARIND RECADO

SERVES 4

FOR RECADO
3 tbsp tamarind paste
1 chipotle in adobo, seeded and
** finely chopped**
3 garlic cloves, crushed

ESSENTIAL EQUIPMENT
4 - 25cm (10in) presoaked bamboo skewers

1 tsp salt
1 tsp dark brown sugar
20 raw tiger prawns, peeled
1 recipe pineapple lime salsa
** (see page 134)**

PRAWN VARIATION
SPICY LIME PRAWNS
Omit tamarind recado and replace with
2 crushed garlic cloves, 1 tsp paprika,
½ tsp chilli powder, 1 tbsp lime juice,
1 tsp salt. Marinate, skewer and grill
prawns according to recipe opposite.
Serve with pineapple lime salsa
or lime wedges.

For recado, combine tamarind paste, chipotle, garlic, salt and sugar. Add prawns and toss to coat evenly. Thread 5 prawns onto each presoaked skewer. Cover with cling film and refrigerate for 30 minutes. Grill according to instructions below. Serve with pineapple lime salsa.

OUTDOOR
Grill over medium-hot coals until the shell is pink and the flesh is opaque, 3 minutes per side.

INDOOR
Preheat overhead grill. Grill until the shell is pink and the flesh is opaque, 3 minutes per side.

THINK AHEAD
Marinate prawns up to 2 hours in advance. Cover and refrigerate.

COOKS' NOTE
Dark, shiny tamarind paste - sometimes referred to as concentrate - has a refreshing, sharp citrus flavour (see page 159). It can be found in most Asian and Middle-Eastern stores. If you can't find the paste, use tamarind pulp. For this recipe, dissolve 3 tbsp pulp in 3 tbsp boiling water, then cool and sieve before using.

BABY SQUID STUFFED WITH CORIANDER AND PICKLED GINGER

SERVES 4

12 baby squid, about 7.5cm (3in) long, cleaned (see opposite)
1 tbsp shoyu (Japanese soy sauce)
1 tbsp sunflower oil
½ tsp black pepper

12 pieces Japanese pickled ginger
2 tbsp fresh coriander leaves
2 garlic cloves, finely sliced
extra shoyu to drizzle

ESSENTIAL EQUIPMENT
24 - 25cm (10in) presoaked bamboo skewers

Combine squid, shoyu, oil and pepper. Toss to coat evenly.
Place 1 piece pickled ginger, a few coriander leaves and 1 garlic slice inside each tube. Insert the tentacles into the tubes. Thread 2 skewers through each squid to secure tentacles to tubes. Grill according to instructions below. Drizzle with shoyu. Serve hot.

OUTDOOR
Grill over medium-hot coals until just opaque, 1-2 minutes per side.

INDOOR
Preheat a ridged cast iron grill pan over high heat. Grill until just opaque, 1-2 minutes per side.

THINK AHEAD
Prepare squid up to 2 hours in advance. Cover with cling film and refrigerate.

COOKS' NOTE
If you don't have pickled ginger, you can use fresh ginger instead. Grate a 1cm (½in) piece of ginger and divide evenly among squid tubes.

CLEANING SQUID
Pull the body from the head and tentacles. Pull out the plastic-like quill. Reserve body tube.

Cut the tentacles from the head in front of the eyes. Squeeze the "beak" from the tentacles and discard, reserving tentacles.

Peel the purple skin from the body tubes and tentacles. Wash the tubes under cold running water.

COOKS' NOTE
Cleaning squid may look daunting and messy, but it's a surprisingly quick and easy process.

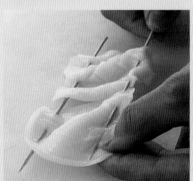

OPENING CLEANED SQUID TUBES
With a small, sharp knife, slit down
one side of the tube and spread flat.

SCORING SQUID
Score inner side with parallel lines
about 1cm (½in) apart to make cross
hatch pattern.

SKEWERING SQUID
Cut squid into 7.5cm (3in) pieces.
Thread strips across parallel skewers.

COOKS' NOTE
Squid needs to be cooked either very quickly over
high heat or very slowly over low heat, to avoid a
tough rubbery texture. When grilling squid, be sure
to remove it from the grill as soon as it is done.

SQUID WITH TOMATO AVOCADO SALSA

SERVES 4

FOR SALSA
4 tomatoes, seeded and diced
1 avocado, diced
3 spring onions, finely chopped
1 fresh green chilli, seeded and finely
  chopped
1 tbsp finely chopped coriander
1 garlic clove, crushed

4 tbsp lime juice
3 tbsp olive oil

350g (12oz) large squid tubes, 25cm
  (10in) long, cleaned (see page 68)
1 tbsp olive oil
salt, black pepper

ESSENTIAL EQUIPMENT
8 - 25cm (10in) presoaked bamboo skewers

For salsa, combine tomatoes, avocado, spring onion, chilli, coriander, garlic, lime
juice and oil. Add salt and pepper to taste.
Open and score squid tubes (see opposite). Toss in oil. Thread on to skewers (see
opposite). Grill according to instructions below. Cut grilled squid into 1cm (½in)
strips. Combine squid strips with salsa. Add salt and pepper to taste. Serve hot or at
room temperature.

OUTDOOR
Grill over medium-hot coals until just opaque,
2 minutes per side.

THINK AHEAD
Make salsa up to 3 hours in advance. Cover tightly with cling film and refrigerate.

INDOOR
Preheat a ridged cast iron grill pan over high heat.
Grill until just opaque, 2 minutes per side.

SPICY MARINATED SQUID ON BRUSCHETTA

SERVES 4

350g (12oz) large squid tubes, 25cm
  (10in) long, cleaned (see page 68)
1 tbsp olive oil
½ red onion, finely chopped
1 garlic clove, crushed
½ tsp crushed chilli flakes
2 tbsp olive oil

1 tbsp lemon juice
2 tomatoes, seeded and diced
1 tbsp chopped fresh mint
salt, black pepper
8 - 1cm (½in) thick slices of day-old
  ciabatta or country-style bread

ESSENTIAL EQUIPMENT
8 – 25cm (10in) presoaked bamboo skewers

Open and score squid tubes (see page 69). Toss squid in 1 tbsp olive oil and skewer
(see page 69). Grill squid according to instructions below. Cut grilled squid into 1cm
(½in) wide strips. Combine onion, garlic, chilli flakes, olive oil, lemon juice, tomatoes
and mint in a bowl. Add squid and toss to coat evenly. Leave at room temperature
for 30 minutes. Toast bread until crisp and striped, 2 minutes per side. Top with
squid. Serve at room temperature or chilled.

OUTDOOR
Grill over medium-hot coals until just opaque,
1-2 minutes per side.

INDOOR
Preheat a ridged cast iron grill pan over high heat.
Grill until just opaque, 1-2 minutes per side.

THINK AHEAD
Grill and marinate squid up to 1 day in advance. Cover and refrigerate.

LEMON CHARMOULA SQUID

SERVES 4

350g (12oz) large squid tubes, 25cm
  (10in) long, cleaned (see page 68)
1 tbsp olive oil
1 recipe charmoula (see page 23)
1 lemon, peeled and chopped
  (see page 161)
salt, black pepper

ESSENTIAL EQUIPMENT
16 - 25cm (10in) presoaked bamboo skewers

Open and score squid tubes (see page
69). Cut scored tubes in to 6 pieces. Toss
in olive oil. Thread on to parallel
skewers (see page 69), with 3 pieces per
pair of skewers. Grill according to
instructions below. Combine charmoula
with lemon. Toss squid with charmoula
and lemon to coat. Sprinkle with salt and
pepper. Serve hot, at room temperature,
or chilled.

OUTDOOR
Grill over medium-hot
coals until just opaque,
2 minutes per side.

INDOOR
Preheat a ridged cast iron
grill pan over high heat.
Grill until just opaque,
2 minutes per side.

THINK AHEAD
Grill squid and combine with charmoula and lemon
up to 1 day in advance. Cover and refrigerate.

COOKS' NOTE
For an authentic Moroccan flavour, use 1 finely
chopped preserved lemon in place of the fresh
lemon. Preserved lemons are available from Middle-
Eastern and gourmet stores (see page 167).

CHARGRILLED LOBSTER WITH GARLIC PARSLEY BUTTER

SERVES 4

4 large cooked lobsters
125g (4oz) garlic parsley butter (see page 140), melted
lemon wedges

Cut lobster in half with a large sharp knife. Scoop out the head sac and discard. Grill according to instructions below. Serve warm with lemon wedges and remaining butter.

OUTDOOR
Grill shell side down over medium-hot coals, frequently brushing flesh with butter, until warmed through, 5 minutes.

INDOOR
Preheat overhead grill. Grill flesh side up, brushing with butter, until warmed through, 5 minutes.

THINK AHEAD
Split lobsters up to 2 hours in advance. Cover and refrigerate.

COOKS' NOTE
Coriander chilli butter (see page 140) in place of the garlic parsley butter, and lime wedges in place of lemon wedges make an excellent alternative recipe for this grilled lobster.

FLAME-ROAST LOBSTER

SERVES 4

4 large cooked lobsters
1 recipe roast garlic aïoli (see page 143)
lemon wedges

OUTDOOR
Grill whole lobster over medium coals until hot to the touch, 5 minutes per side. Bash open and serve warm with roast garlic aïoli and lemon wedges.

CUTTING A LOBSTER IN HALF
Place the lobster belly side down. Insert the tip of a large knife at the cross mark right behind the head and cut through the head (see above). Turn the lobster round. Holding it firmly by the head, cut it in half lengthwise from head to tail.

CLAMS IN CORIANDER CHILLI BUTTER

SERVES 4

2kg (4lb) clams
125g (4oz) coriander chilli butter (see page 140), melted

Scrub clams under running water. Discard any that are broken or not tightly closed. To cook outdoors, fold 1 metre of foil in half for double thickness. Spread clams over middle of foil. Fold in the edges to make a parcel. To cook indoors, put clams in a large dry pan and cover. Grill or cook according to instructions below. Pour over the melted butter and remove from the heat when butter is hot and fragrant, 1 minute. Serve hot, discarding any clams that have not opened.

OUTDOOR
Grill over medium-low coals until shells are open and the clams turn opaque, 8-10 minutes. Open the foil out but leave the edges raised so that no juices escape.

INDOOR
Cook over medium heat until shells open and the clams turn opaque, 6 minutes. Shake pan occasionally to ensure even cooking.

MUSSELS IN BEER AND GARLIC

SERVES 4

2kg (4lb) mussels
100ml (3½ floz) lager
2 garlic cloves, finely chopped
2 tbsp chopped flat-leaf parsley
salt, black pepper

Scrub mussels under running water. Discard any that are broken or not tightly closed. To cook outdoors, fold 1 metre of foil in half for double thickness. Spread mussels over middle of foil. Scrunch up the edges of the foil and pour over the lager. Fold up edges to make a parcel. To cook indoors, put mussels and lager in a large pan with a lid on. Grill or cook according to instructions below. Sprinkle with the garlic and parsley. Remove from heat when you can smell the garlic, 1 minute. Sprinkle with salt and pepper. Serve hot, discarding any mussels that have not opened.

OUTDOOR
Grill over medium-low coals until shells are open and the mussels turn opaque, 8-10 minutes. Open the foil but leave the edges raised so no juices escape.

INDOOR
Steam over medium heat until shells are open and the mussels turn opaque, 6 minutes. Shake pan occasionally to ensure even cooking.

FISH ESSENTIALS

GOLDEN RULE FOR COOKING FISH
Never desert your post once fish is placed on the grill. Fish is naturally tender. Most fish requires only brief grilling to firm its flesh and to bring out its delicate flavour. Overcooked fish is dry and tasteless, and overcooking can happen in a matter of minutes.

SELECTING FISH FOR THE GRILL
• Oil rich fish with a firm meaty texture is the easiest to grill. This includes salmon, tuna, halibut, swordfish, snapper and mackerel.
• Skin left on fish acts to protect the delicate flesh and turns deliciously crisp on the grill.
• Firm textured flesh also means that the fish will hold together better.

GETTING IT READY
• Cut deep slashes through the skin side of fish fillets and through to the bone of whole fish to allow flavour, smoke and heat to penetrate evenly.
• Liberal oiling is important for all types of fish to prevent it from drying out, except in the case of very oily skinned fish, like sardines.

MARINATING
• Fish requires only a very brief amount of time in a marinade. Tender fish flesh absorbs a marinade faster than the denser flesh of red meat. When left in an acidic marinade for too long, fish flesh will literally start to cook and turn white.

• Marinate fish for no longer than 2 hours in the refrigerator. It is better to drizzle or brush an oil rich flavour mix over the fish flesh than give it a long soak in a wet acidic marinade.

PUTTING IT ON
• Before putting fish on the grill make sure to bring it to room temperature. Remove it from the refrigerator no more than 30 minutes beforehand. This will ensure that it cooks evenly and quickly.
• Use a hinged grill rack to turn fish that is tender and delicate. It will help to keep whole fish intact and prevent fillets from breaking apart.
• When turning fish with a metal spatula, turn only once, to stop the fish from falling apart.

TAKING IT OFF
Fish will continue cooking a significant amount after it is removed from the grill. To avoid overcooked, dry and flavourless fish, remove as soon as it is done. You can always put it back on but once it is overcooked there is no quick fix. Fish is done when it is opaque through to the centre but still moist and tender. Cook fish until the internal temperature reads 60°C (140°F).

FINAL FLAVOURING
• Salting raw fish draws out moisture and toughens the flesh. Always add seasoning after cooking but be sure not to forget.

• Add complementary flavours and moisture after removing it from the grill with sauces, salsas and dressings (consult pages 130-143 for more ideas).

CHARGRILLED SWORDFISH WITH ROAST PEPPER AND BASIL SALSA

SERVES 4

4 -175g (6oz) swordfish steaks
1 tbsp olive oil
salt, black pepper

1 recipe roast pepper and basil salsa
(see page 138)

ESSENTIAL EQUIPMENT
hinged wire rack, or alternatively a long metal spatula for turning fish on the grill

Brush the steaks with olive oil on both sides. Grill according to instructions below.
Sprinkle with salt and pepper. Spoon over salsa and serve hot.

OUTDOOR
Grill over medium-hot coals until just opaque,
3 minutes per side.

INDOOR
Preheat a ridged cast iron grill pan over high heat.
Grill until just opaque, 3 minutes per side.

COOKS' NOTE
Salsa fresca (see page 133), coriander coconut sauce (see page 138), salsa verde (see page 134) and chilli
lime mayonnaise (see page 143) all complement swordfish wonderfully. Shark, salmon, halibut or monkfish
make excellent alternatives to swordfish with this simple, no-frills preparation.

SPICE-CRUSTED TUNA WITH THAI CITRUS DRESSING

SERVES 4

4 - 200g (7oz) tuna fillets,
  2.5cm (1in) thick
1 tbsp sunflower oil
2 tbsp coriander seeds
2 tbsp black peppercorns
lime wedges

FOR DRESSING
2 lemon grass stalks
1 fresh red chilli, seeded and finely
  sliced
1 tbsp finely chopped fresh coriander
2 tbsp fish sauce
2 tbsp sunflower oil
6 tbsp lime juice

ESSENTIAL EQUIPMENT
hinged wire rack, or alternatively a long metal spatula for turning fish on the grill

For dressing, remove and discard the tough outer skin from the lemon grass stalks and finely slice. Combine lemon grass, chilli, fresh coriander, fish sauce, oil and lime juice. Brush fillets on both sides with oil. Crush the coriander seeds and peppercorns (see page 161). Press crushed seeds on to both sides of fillets. Grill according to instructions below. Pour over dressing and serve hot or at room temperature with lime wedges.

OUTDOOR
Grill over hot coals, 2 minutes per side for rare, 3 minutes per side for medium rare, 4 minutes per side for well done.

INDOOR
Preheat a ridged cast iron grill pan over high heat. Grill for 2 minutes per side for rare, 3 minutes per side for medium rare, 4 minutes per side for well done.

THINK AHEAD
Coat tuna with spices up to 4 hours in advance. Cover and refrigerate. Make dressing up to 3 hours in advance. Cover and refrigerate.

COOKS' NOTE
Salsa fresca (see page 133), creamy avocado salsa (see page 132), roast pepper and basil salsa (see page 138), or avocado mango salsa (see page 136) are all delicious served with this simple tuna recipe.

CHARGRILLED SARDINES

SERVES 4

24 - 30g (1oz) ungutted small
  sardines
salt, black pepper

ESSENTIAL EQUIPMENT
hinged wire rack

Grill sardines according to instructions below. Sprinkle with salt and pepper. Serve hot with lemon wedges.

OUTDOOR
Place sardines in hinged wire rack. Grill over medium-hot coals until opaque throughout and crispy on the outside, 3 minutes per side.

INDOOR
Don't even attempt to grill sardines indoors, unless you are planning to move house. The aroma will linger forever!

COOKS' NOTE
If you grill large sardines they will need cleaning and gutting. Allow 3 sardines per person. Grill for 5 minutes per side.

CHARGRILLED SEA BASS WITH FENNEL, LEMON AND OLIVE OIL

SERVES 4

4 - 175g (6oz) unskinned sea bass
  fillets
1 fennel bulb, grated
4 garlic cloves, finely sliced
2 tbsp chopped flat-leaf parsley
1½ tsp salt
1 tsp black pepper
1 tsp fennel seeds
1 tbsp olive oil
1 lemon, sliced
1 recipe salsa verde (see page 134),
  optional

ESSENTIAL EQUIPMENT
4 – 40cm (16in) squares heavy duty foil

Cut several shallow diagonal slashes about 2.5cm (1in) apart on the skin side of each fillet. Divide the fennel, garlic and parsley among the foil squares, spreading in an even layer on one half of each foil piece. Place the fish skin side up on top. Sprinkle with salt, pepper and fennel seeds. Drizzle over oil. Place lemon slices on top. Fold over the other half of the foil. Fold over edges to seal foil packets tightly. Grill or bake according to instructions below. Serve hot in foil packet with salsa verde.

OUTDOOR
Grill over medium-hot coals until fish is opaque throughout, 8-10 minutes. Flip foil packet over half way through grilling.

INDOOR
Preheat oven to 200°C (400°F) gas 6. Bake until fish is opaque throughout, 8-10 minutes

THINK AHEAD
Prepare foil packets up to 2 hours in advance. Refrigerate.

COOKS' NOTE
Sea bream, grey mullet, grouper or red snapper fillets make good alternatives to sea bass in this fennel-fragrant recipe.

HERBED SALMON WITH TOMATO VINAIGRETTE

SERVES 4

2 - 350g (12oz) tail end salmon fillets
juice of 1 lemon
2 tbsp finely chopped fresh dill
2 tsp salt
1 tsp black pepper
½ tsp coriander seeds, crushed
  (see page 161)

ESSENTIAL EQUIPMENT
hinged grill rack

FOR VINAIGRETTE
1 garlic clove, crushed
1 shallot, finely chopped
2 tbsp red wine vinegar
4 tbsp olive oil
3 tomatoes, seeded and diced
salt, black pepper

For vinaigrette, combine garlic, shallot and vinegar. Leave to stand for 30 minutes. Whisk in the oil and tomatoes. Add salt and pepper to taste. Place salmon fillets skin side down. Drizzle lemon juice evenly over both fillets. Sprinkle 1 salmon fillet with dill, salt, pepper and coriander seeds. Place uncoated fillet skin side up over the other fillet. Grill according to instructions below. Cut into four portions. Spoon over vinaigrette and serve hot.

OUTDOOR
Place sandwiched fillets in hinged grill rack. Grill over medium-hot coals until skin is very crisp and flesh has just turned opaque but is still moist and pink in the centre, 5 minutes per side.

INDOOR
Preheat oven to 200°C (400°F) gas 6. Place sandwiched fillets on rack in roasting tin. Roast until flesh has just turned opaque but is still moist and pink in the centre, 15-20 minutes.

THINK AHEAD
Sandwich fillets together up to 2 hours in advance. Cover tightly with cling film and refrigerate. Make vinaigrette up to 6 hours in advance. Cover and refrigerate.

MOROCCAN SPICED MACKEREL

SERVES 4

4 - 375g (13oz) whole mackerel
1 recipe charmoula (see page 23)
salt, black pepper

ESSENTIAL EQUIPMENT
hinged wire rack, or alternatively a long metal spatula for turning fish on the grill

Cut slashes about 5cm (2in) apart down both sides of each fish, cutting through to the bones. Spread ½ tbsp of the charmoula down both sides of the inside cavity of each fish. Grill according to instructions below. Sprinkle with salt and pepper. Serve hot with the remaining charmoula.

OUTDOOR
Grill over medium-hot coals until flesh is opaque at the bone and skin is very crispy, 5 minutes per side.

INDOOR
Preheat overhead grill. Grill until the flesh is opaque at the bone and the skin is very crispy, 5 minutes per side.

THINK AHEAD
Prepare mackerel for grilling up to 2 hours in advance. Cover tightly with cling film and refrigerate.

COOKS' NOTE
Chimi churri sauce (see page 135) used as an alternative to the charmoula is also very good for flavouring mackerel.

WASABI SOY SALMON WITH SESAME SOBA NOODLES

SERVES 4

4 -175g (6oz) salmon fillets
1 tsp wasabi paste
2 tsp brown sugar
1 tbsp sake

1 tbsp lime juice
3 tbsp shoyu (Japanese soy sauce)
1 recipe sesame soba noodle salad (see page 148)

ESSENTIAL EQUIPMENT
hinged wire rack, or alternatively a long metal spatula for turning fish on the grill

Combine wasabi, sugar, sake, lime and shoyu. Set aside 2 tbsp for drizzling. Brush the fillets on both sides with the remaining mixture. Grill according to instructions below. Serve hot with sesame soba noodle salad and drizzle over reserved mixture.

OUTDOOR
Grill over medium-hot coals until the flesh just turns opaque but is still moist and pink in the middle, 3-4 minutes per side.

INDOOR
Preheat a ridged cast iron grill pan over high heat. Grill until the flesh just turns opaque but is still moist and pink in the middle, 3-4 minutes per side.

THINK AHEAD
Brush the salmon up to 30 minutes in advance.

CHARGRILLED TROUT WITH GARLIC PARSLEY BUTTER

SERVES 4

4 - 250g (8oz) trout without head, butterflied (see opposite)
1 tbsp sunflower oil
salt, black pepper
lemon wedges
4 - 1cm (½in) slices garlic parsley butter (see page 140)

ESSENTIAL EQUIPMENT
hinged wire rack, or alternatively a long metal spatula for turning fish on the grill

Brush flesh side of trout with oil. Place trout in hinged wire rack, if using. Grill according to instructions below. Sprinkle with salt and pepper. Serve hot with garlic parsley butter and lemon wedges.

OUTDOOR
Grill skin side down over medium-hot coals until skin starts to turn crisp, 2 minutes. Turn and grill for 1 minute. Turn again. Grill until flesh just turns opaque, is firm, and the skin is crispy, a further 2 minutes.

INDOOR
Preheat overhead grill. Grill skin side up until skin starts to turn crispy, 2 minutes. Turn and grill for 1 minute. Turn again. Grill until flesh just turns opaque, is firm, and the skin is crispy, a further 2 minutes.

THINK AHEAD
Butterfly trout up to 8 hours in advance. Cover tightly with cling film and refrigerate.

BUTTERFLYING TROUT
Lay a gutted, headless trout skin side down on a cutting board. Working down one side, slide the tip of a sharp knife between the rib bones and flesh. Use small stroking cuts to release the bones. Repeat on the opposite side.

Place fish skin side down and open flat. Lift up backbone from head to tail and cut off with scissors.

RED SNAPPER TACOS WITH CHILLI LIME MAYO

SERVES 4

4 - 175g (6oz) unskinned red snapper
  fillets
1 garlic clove, crushed
½ tsp ground cumin
½ tsp chilli powder
½ tsp dried oregano
1 tbsp lime juice
2 tbsp olive oil
salt, black pepper
4 - 20cm (8in) flour tortillas or fresh
  corn tortillas
1 avocado, diced
2 tbsp fresh coriander leaves
1 recipe chilli lime mayonnaise
  (see page 143)

ESSENTIAL EQUIPMENT
*hinged wire rack, or alternatively a long metal
spatula for turning fish on the grill*

Combine the garlic, cumin, chilli powder,
oregano, lime juice and oil. Brush
mixture over fillets. Place fillets in
hinged wire rack, if using. Grill fillets
according to instructions below. Sprinkle
with salt and pepper. Warm tortillas
directly over the grill or in the hot grill
pan for 30 seconds each side. Cut fish
into 4cm (1½in) cubes. Divide among
warmed tortillas. Top with avocado dice,
coriander leaves and chilli lime
mayonnaise. Fold in half and serve hot.

OUTDOOR
Grill fillets over medium-
hot coals, skin side down
for 3 minutes. Turn and
grill until opaque
throughout, a further
3 minutes.

INDOOR
Preheat a ridged cast
iron grill pan. Grill fillets
skin side down for 3
minutes. Turn and grill
until opaque throughout,
a further 3 minutes.

THINK AHEAD
Brush the snapper with seasoning up to 30 minutes
in advance.

COOKS' NOTE
Red mullet, grouper or sea bass fillets are excellent
alternatives to red snapper.

ALTERNATIVE SEAFOOD FOR PROVENÇAL GRILLADE

Feel free to make any of the following substitutions:

4 cooked, cracked lobster claws, in place of crab.

2 - 175g (6oz) fillets red snapper, grouper or bass, in place of red and grey mullet fillets.

2 - 175 (6oz) salmon or swordfish steaks, in place of tuna.

12 tiger prawns, in place of langoustine.

8 skewered scallops, grilled until just opaque, 2 minutes per side, as an optional addition.

PROVENÇAL SEAFOOD GRILLADE WITH LEMON FENNEL DRESSING AND ROAST GARLIC AÏOLI

SERVES 4 - 6

2 garlic cloves, crushed
2 tbsp Pernod
2 tbsp olive oil
4 large cooked crab
500g (1lb) tuna fillet,
  2.5cm (1in) thick
2 - 175g (6oz) red mullet fillets
2 - 175g (6oz) grey mullet fillets
8 cooked langoustines

ESSENTIAL EQUIPMENT
long metal spatula

FOR DRESSING
6 tbsp olive oil
2 tbsp lemon juice
2 tbsp red wine vinegar
1 tbsp finely chopped fresh fennel
  or dill
salt, black pepper

1 recipe roast garlic aïoli
  (see page 143)
crusty bread and lemon wedges

For dressing, whisk oil into lemon and vinegar. Stir in fennel or dill. Add salt and pepper to taste. Combine garlic, Pernod and oil. Using a hammer or rolling pin, crack crab or lobster claws just enough to expose the interior to seasoning. Brush all the seafood with the garlic mixture. Grill according to instructions below. Cut cooked tuna and fish fillets into chunks. Arrange seafood on platter. Drizzle over dressing. Serve hot or at room temperature with roast garlic aïoli, crusty bread and lemon wedges.

OUTDOOR
Grill seafood over medium-hot coals, using spatula to turn. Grill tuna for 3 minutes per side for rare, 4 minutes per side for medium rare, 5 minutes per side for well done. Grill fish fillets, skin side down first, until opaque throughout, 3 minutes per side. Grill shellfish until warmed through, 3 minutes per side.

INDOOR
This recipe is inappropriate for indoor cooking.

THINK AHEAD
Crack and brush seafood up to 2 hours in advance. Cover with cling film and refrigerate.

CHICKEN ESSENTIALS

GETTING IT READY

Chicken should be grilled in pieces of uniform shape and thickness. This is essential to ensure safe, even cooking, and to guarantee the best results.

• De-boning joints (see page 104), splitting and flattening whole birds (see page 110) and butterflying boneless breasts (see page 94) allow chicken to cook evenly and prevent overcooked white meat.

• Slashing (see page 102) and making shallow cuts (see page 92) open the greatest surface area to flavour, smoke and heat. This allows marinades to penetrate more deeply and chicken to cook quickly and evenly.

MARINATING

The intense heat of an outdoor grill can dry out naturally lean chicken meat, especially when it has been de-boned and skinned. Marinating is an essential step to retaining moisture during cooking, but it is also important not to overdo it. Overmarinating will draw moisture out from, toughen, and when acid is present, literally begin to cook the meat. The result is poultry that looks greyish white and rubbery. Marinate for the recommended time only.

PUTTING IT ON

Before putting chicken on the grill make sure to bring it to room temperature, by removing it from the refrigerator no more than 20 minutes beforehand. This will ensure that it cooks evenly and quickly.

Be sure to brush poultry liberally with oil to keep it moist during grilling.

Cooking chicken for a crowd? Get ahead by pre-cooking on the bone chicken pieces (such as wings, drums and whole split birds) in a preheated 200°C (400°F) Gas 6 oven for 15 minutes. Transfer to the grill when your guests arrive and reduce the required cooking time by approximately 10 minutes.

TAKING IT OFF

Check doneness by making a cut into the meat with a small, sharp knife (see page 13), before removing chicken from the grill. It is always better to check doneness at the grill than to discover undercooked meat on the plate. Chicken is done when it is opaque throughout with no trace of pink at the bone.

Watch boneless cuts carefully to avoid overcooking and to ensure maximum juiciness and succulence.

FINAL FLAVOURING

We add salt just before serving because salting any sooner will draw out the chicken's flavourful juices. But don't forget to season before putting food on the table.

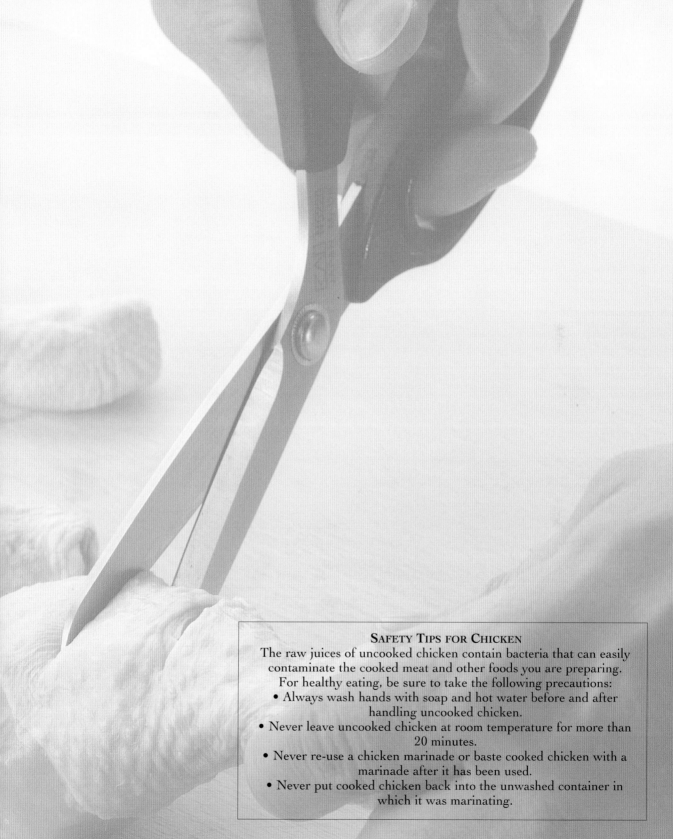

SAFETY TIPS FOR CHICKEN

The raw juices of uncooked chicken contain bacteria that can easily contaminate the cooked meat and other foods you are preparing. For healthy eating, be sure to take the following precautions:

- Always wash hands with soap and hot water before and after handling uncooked chicken.
- Never leave uncooked chicken at room temperature for more than 20 minutes.
- Never re-use a chicken marinade or baste cooked chicken with a marinade after it has been used.
- Never put cooked chicken back into the unwashed container in which it was marinating.

SLASHING CHICKEN BREASTS
With a sharp knife, cut 3 parallel slashes through skin, about 0.5cm (¼in) deep.

COOKS' NOTE
We slash the chicken breasts to allow the flavours of the seasonings and marinades to penetrate the chicken more fully.

CITRUS RECADO CHICKEN BREASTS

SERVES 4

2 garlic cloves, crushed
1 tsp chilli powder
½ tsp dried oregano
½ tsp dried thyme
½ tsp ground cumin
½ tsp ground coriander
½ tsp black pepper
¼ tsp ground cinnamon
1 tbsp dark brown sugar

2 tbsp sunflower oil
2 tbsp lime juice
4 tbsp orange juice
4 boneless chicken breasts, slashed
   (see opposite)
salt
1 recipe avocado mango salsa
   (see page 136), optional

Combine garlic, chilli powder, oregano, thyme, cumin, coriander, pepper, cinnamon, sugar, oil, lime juice and orange juice. Add chicken and toss to coat evenly. Cover and refrigerate for 30 minutes, turning once. Grill according to instructions below. Sprinkle with salt. Serve hot with avocado mango salsa, optional.

OUTDOOR
Grill skin side down over medium-hot coals until skin is crisp, 7 minutes. Turn and continue grilling until chicken is opaque with no trace of pink, a further 5 minutes.

INDOOR
Preheat overhead grill. Grill skin side up until skin is crisp, 7 minutes. Turn and continue grilling until chicken is opaque with no trace of pink, a further 5 minutes.

THINK AHEAD
Marinate chicken up to 2 hours in advance. Cover and refrigerate, turning several times in marinade.

COOKS' NOTE
We prefer the mildly spicy sweet heat of ancho chilli powder in this Mexican-style dish. These wrinkled reddish brown chillies are actually dried poblanos. They are widely used in Mexican cooking. For complete authenticity, also try to find dried Mexican oregano. Both are available from speciality shops or gourmet mail order sources (see page 167).

HERBED BALSAMIC CHICKEN BREASTS

SERVES 4

2 garlic cloves, crushed
1 tsp herbes de Provence
½ tsp black pepper
1 tbsp creamy dijon mustard
1 tbsp olive oil
4 tbsp balsamic vinegar
salt, black pepper
4 boneless chicken breasts, slashed (see page 92)
1 recipe roast red pepper aïoli (see page 143), optional

Combine garlic, herbes de Provence, pepper, mustard, oil and vinegar. Add chicken and toss to coat evenly. Cover and refrigerate for 30 minutes, turning once. Grill according to instructions below. Sprinkle with salt and pepper. Serve hot with roast red pepper aïoli, optional.

OUTDOOR
Grill skin side down on medium-hot coals until crisp, 7 minutes. Turn and continue grilling until chicken is opaque with no trace of pink, a further 5 minutes.

INDOOR
Preheat overhead grill. Grill skin side up until skin is crisp, about 7 minutes. Turn and continue grilling until chicken is opaque with no trace of pink, a further 5 minutes.

THINK AHEAD
Marinate chicken breasts up to 2 hours in advance. Cover and refrigerate, turning every 15 to 20 minutes.

COOKS' NOTE
Herbes de Provence, a fragrant dry herb mix that includes fennel, lavender and summer savoury, is a kitchen cupboard essential. Sprinkle over poultry, meats, fish or vegetables to bring the scent and flavour of sun-soaked Provence into your kitchen.

GINGER SOY CHICKEN BREASTS

SERVES 4

2 tbsp grated fresh ginger
3 garlic cloves, crushed
2 tbsp dark brown sugar
2 tsp sesame seeds
2 tsp toasted sesame oil
1 tbsp medium dry sherry
8 tbsp soy sauce
4 boneless chicken breasts, slashed (see page 92)
salt, black pepper
1 recipe coriander coconut sauce (see page 138), optional

Combine ginger, garlic, sugar, sesame seeds, sesame oil, sherry and soy sauce. Add chicken and toss to coat evenly. Cover and refrigerate for 30 minutes, turning once. Grill according to instructions below. Sprinkle with salt and pepper. Serve hot with coriander coconut sauce, optional.

OUTDOOR
Grill skin side down on medium-hot coals until crisp, 7 minutes. Turn and continue grilling until chicken is opaque with no trace of pink, a further 5 minutes.

INDOOR
Preheat overhead grill. Grill skin side up until skin is crisp, 7 minutes. Turn and continue grilling until chicken is opaque with no trace of pink, a further 5 minutes.

THINK AHEAD
Marinate chicken breasts up to 2 hours in advance. Cover and refrigerate, turning every 15-20 minutes.

BUTTERFLYING CHICKEN BREAST
With one hand on the breast to hold it in place, slice through the middle horizontally to cut almost in half. Open out flat.

THINK AHEAD
Butterfly breast up to 1 day in advance. Cover tightly with cling film and refrigerate.

COOKS' NOTE
Butterflying makes chicken breasts into thin fillets that can be cooked in a flash. It also produces the perfect pocket for stuffing.

THAI LIME AND COCONUT CHICKEN

SERVES 4

2 lemon grass stalks
3 fresh green chillies, seeded and
  chopped
2 garlic cloves, chopped
3 spring onions, chopped
1 handful fresh coriander leaves
½ tsp ground cumin
½ tsp ground white pepper
½ tsp turmeric
1 tsp ground coriander

grated zest 1 lime
3 tbsp lime juice
2 tsp grated fresh ginger
1 tbsp fish sauce
125ml (4floz) coconut milk
4 boneless, skinless chicken breasts,
  butterflied (see opposite)
salt, black pepper
1 recipe fresh papaya sambal (see
  page 137), optional

Remove and discard the tough outer skin from the lemon grass stalks and roughly chop. Put lemon grass, chillies, garlic, spring onion, fresh coriander, cumin, pepper, turmeric, ground coriander, lime zest, lime juice, ginger, fish sauce and coconut milk in food processor or blender; pulse until smooth. In a bowl, toss chicken with lemon grass mixture. Cover and refrigerate for 1 hour. Grill according to instructions below. Sprinkle with salt and pepper. Serve hot with fresh papaya sambal, optional.

OUTDOOR
Grill over medium hot coals until the chicken is opaque, with no trace of pink, 3 minutes per side.

INDOOR
Preheat overhead grill. Grill until the chicken is opaque with no trace of pink, 3 minutes per side.

THINK AHEAD
Make marinade up to 3 days in advance. Cover and refrigerate. Marinate chicken up to 4 hours in advance. Cover and refrigerate.

LEMON OREGANO CHICKEN BAGUETTE

SERVES 4

4 boneless, skinless chicken breasts,
  butterflied (see page 94)
1 lemon, peeled and chopped
  (see page 161)
2 garlic cloves, crushed
2 tsp dried oregano
2 tbsp olive oil

1 tsp black pepper
1 baguette
salt
1 beefsteak tomato, sliced
1 handful crisp salad leaves
1 recipe roast garlic aïoli
  (see page 143)

Toss chicken breasts with lemon, garlic, oregano, oil and pepper. Cover and
refrigerate for 20 minutes. Cut baguette into 4 equal-sized pieces. Split and toast
baguette on the cut side until just crisp, 1 minute. Grill chicken according to
instructions below. Sprinkle with salt. Fill baguette with tomatoes, salad, chicken
and aïoli. Serve warm.

OUTDOOR
Grill over medium hot coals until chicken is opaque,
with no trace of pink, 3 minutes per side.

INDOOR
Preheat overhead grill. Grill until the chicken is
opaque with no trace of pink, 3 minutes per side.

THINK AHEAD
Marinate chicken up to 2 hours in advance. Cover and refrigerate, turning in the marinade every 15-20 minutes.

CHICKEN, PROSCIUTTO AND SAGE SKEWERS

SERVES 4

4 boneless, skinless chicken breasts
1 garlic clove, crushed
1 tsp black pepper
2 tbsp lemon juice
2 tbsp olive oil
12 fresh sage leaves
6 slices prosciutto, cut in half
4 - 2.5cm (1in) cubes country style
day-old bread
1 recipe roast red pepper aïoli
(see page 143)

ESSENTIAL EQUIPMENT
4 - 35cm (14in) flat metal skewers

Cut each breast lengthwise into 3 strips. Combine garlic, pepper, lemon juice and oil. Add chicken strips and toss to coat evenly. Place one sage leaf on top of each prosciutto half slice. Place one chicken strip on top of the sage. Roll up prosciutto and sage around each chicken strip. Thread 3 wrapped strips lengthwise on to each skewer. Toss bread cubes in 1 tbsp olive oil. Thread 1 bread cube on to the end of each skewer. Grill according to instructions below. Serve hot with roast red pepper aïoli.

OUTDOOR
Grill over medium-hot coals, turning every 2 minutes, until cooked through, 8-10 minutes.

INDOOR
Preheat overhead grill. Grill, turning every 2 minutes, until cooked through, 8-10 minutes.

THINK AHEAD
Skewer chicken but not bread up to 6 hours in advance. Cover and refrigerate. Toss and skewer bread cubes just before grilling.

SKEWERED BAJAAN CHICKEN

SERVES 4

2 garlic cloves
4 spring onions
½ red onion
½ scotch bonnet chilli, seeded or
1 fresh red chilli, seeded
1 handful flat-leaf parsley
1 tsp fresh thyme leaves
2 tbsp lime juice

2 tbsp sunflower oil
¼ tsp ground allspice
salt, black pepper
4 boneless chicken breasts,
butterflied (see page 94)
1 recipe creamy avocado salsa
(see page 132), optional

ESSENTIAL EQUIPMENT
4 - 25cm (10in) presoaked bamboo skewers

Place garlic, spring onion, red onion, chilli, parsley, thyme, lime juice, oil and allspice in a food processor or blender; pulse to a paste. Add salt and pepper to taste. Open out chicken breasts and spread 1 tbsp paste on each opened breast. Fold breasts over again. Thread a skewer through cut edges of breast, weaving in and out several times to hold the chicken edges together. Grill according to instructions below. Sprinkle with salt and pepper. Serve hot with creamy avocado salsa, optional.

OUTDOOR
Grill skin side down over medium-hot coals until skin is crisp, 7 minutes. Turn and continue grilling until chicken is opaque with no trace of pink, a further 5 minutes.

INDOOR
Preheat overhead grill. Grill skin side up until skin is crisp, 7 minutes. Turn and continue grilling until chicken is opaque with no trace of pink, a further 5 minutes.

THINK AHEAD
Stuff breasts up to 1 day in advance. Wrap in cling film and refrigerate.

COOKS' NOTE
Butterflying a chicken breast produces a perfect pocket for stuffing. As an alternative to bajaan stuffing, substitute charmoula (see page 23), spicy jerk rub (see page 24) or the simple combination of crushed garlic and chopped fresh herbs.

SWEET CHILLI CHICKEN

SERVES 4

4 boneless, skinless chicken breasts
1 fresh red chilli, seeded and
  finely chopped
2 garlic cloves, crushed
1 tbsp grated fresh ginger
4 tbsp runny honey
2 tbsp soy sauce
4 tbsp lime juice

FOR GARNISHES

1 spring onion, diagonally sliced
1 fresh red chilli, seeded and
  finely sliced
1 tbsp fresh mint leaves
1 tbsp fresh coriander leaves

ESSENTIAL EQUIPMENT
4 - 35cm (14in) flat metal skewers

Cut each breast lengthwise into 3 strips. Combine chilli, garlic, ginger, honey, soy sauce and lime juice. Reserve 4 tbsp mixture. Add chicken to remaining mixture and toss to coat evenly. Cover and refrigerate for 30 minutes. Thread 3 chicken strips on to each skewer. Grill according to instructions below. Drizzle over reserved sweet chilli mixture. Sprinkle with spring onion, chilli, mint and coriander leaves. Serve hot.

OUTDOOR
Grill over medium-hot coals, turning every 2 minutes, until cooked through, 8-10 minutes.

INDOOR
Preheat overhead grill. Grill, turning every 2 minutes, until cooked through, 8-10 minutes.

THINK AHEAD
Marinate chicken up to 2 hours in advance. Cover and refrigerate.

COOKS' NOTE
This is Asian finger food. We also like to wrap up each succulent piece of chicken with its fragrant and spicy garnishes in a crisp, cool lettuce cup.

LEMON YOGHURT CHICKEN WRAP

SERVES 4

4 boneless, skinless chicken breasts
2 garlic cloves, crushed
¼ tsp ground cinnamon
¼ tsp ground allspice
1 tsp black pepper
1 tbsp olive oil
3 tbsp lemon juice
2 tbsp Greek-style yoghurt

4 pitta or flatbreads
1 handful shredded iceberg
  or cos lettuce
4 tomatoes, sliced
8 radishes, sliced
salt
1 recipe roast garlic aïoli
  (see page 143)

ESSENTIAL EQUIPMENT
4 - 35cm (14in) flat metal skewers

Cut each breast lengthwise into 3 strips. Combine garlic, cinnamon, allspice, pepper, oil, lemon juice and yoghurt. Add chicken strips and toss to coat evenly. Cover and refrigerate for 30 minutes. Thread 3 chicken strips on to each skewer. Grill according to instructions below. Split open and separate each warmed pitta into 2 halves. Stack 2 pitta halves cut side up. Using a fork, slide the chicken pieces from 1 skewer on to the pitta. Top with a quarter of the lettuce, tomatoes and radishes. Spoon over aïoli. Add salt and pepper and roll up. Repeat with remaining pitta, chicken, lettuce, tomatoes, radishes and aïoli. Serve hot.

OUTDOOR
Grill over medium-hot coals, turning every 2 minutes, until cooked through, 8-10 minutes. Place pitta halves directly on the grill until just warm, about 30 seconds per side.

INDOOR
Preheat overhead grill. Grill, turning every 2 minutes, until cooked through, 8-10 minutes. Place pitta halves briefly under grill until warm, 15 seconds per side.

THINK AHEAD
Marinate chicken up to 3 hours in advance. Cover and refrigerate.

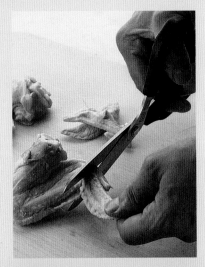

THAI SPICED CHICKEN WINGS

MAKES 20

2 lemon grass stalks
2 tbsp grated fresh ginger
5 garlic cloves, crushed
1 red onion, quartered
grated zest of 1 lime
2 tsp crushed chilli flakes
¹/₂ tsp ground coriander
¹/₂ tsp ground cumin

¹/₂ tsp paprika
2 tsp salt
1 tbsp sunflower oil
6 tbsp dark brown sugar
6 tbsp tomato purée
20 large chicken wings, tips cut off
   (see opposite)

ESSENTIAL EQUIPMENT
8 - 35cm (14in) flat metal skewers

Remove and discard the tough outer skin from the lemon grass stalks and roughly chop. Place lemon grass, ginger, garlic, onion, lime zest, chilli flakes, coriander, cumin, paprika, salt, oil, sugar and tomato purée in a food processor or blender; pulse until smooth. In a bowl, combine the mixture with the wings and toss to coat evenly. Cover and refrigerate for 2 hours. Thread the wings on to parallel skewers (see opposite). Grill according to instructions below. Serve hot.

OUTDOOR
Grill the wings over medium-hot coals for 15-20 minutes, turning every 5 minutes, until the meat at the bone is opaque.

INDOOR
Preheat grill. Arrange the wings on a wire rack over an oven tray. Grill for 15-20 minutes, turning once, until the meat at the bone is opaque.

THINK AHEAD
Marinate the wings up to 8 hours in advance. Make marinade up to 1 week in advance. Cover and refrigerate.

CUTTING OFF WING TIPS
To remove the wing tip, use a sharp pair of kitchen scissors and cut at the joint.

**THREADING CHICKEN WINGS ON
TO SKEWERS**
Make sure that the skewers pass through the middle to secure both joints.

HONEY SOY CHICKEN WINGS

MAKES 20

6 tbsp dark soy sauce
3 tbsp dry sherry
2 tbsp runny honey
20 large chicken wings, tips cut off (see page 100)
1 recipe spicy peanut sauce (see page 136), optional

ESSENTIAL EQUIPMENT

8 - 35cm (14in) flat metal skewers

Combine soy sauce, sherry and honey in a bowl. Add the wings and toss to coat evenly. Cover and refrigerate for 2 hours. Thread the wings on to parallel skewers (see page 100). Grill according to instructions below. Serve hot with spicy peanut sauce, optional.

OUTDOOR
Grill over medium-hot coals for 15-20 minutes, turning every 5 minutes, until the meat at the bone is opaque.

INDOOR
Preheat grill. Arrange the wings on a wire rack over an oven tray. Grill for 15-20 minutes, turning once, until the meat at the bone is opaque.

THINK AHEAD
Marinate the wings up to 8 hours in advance. Cover and refrigerate.

SPICY LIME CHICKEN WINGS

MAKES 20

2 limes, peeled and chopped (see page 161)
2 garlic cloves, crushed
1 tsp chilli powder
1 tsp paprika
2 tsp granulated sugar
20 large chicken wings, tips cut off (see page 100)
2 tsp salt
1 recipe creamy avocado salsa (see page 132), optional

ESSENTIAL EQUIPMENT

8 - 35cm (14in) flat metal skewers

Combine lime flesh, garlic, chilli powder, paprika and sugar in a bowl. Add the wings and toss to coat evenly. Cover and refrigerate for 2 hours. Thread the wings on to parallel skewers (see page 100). Grill according to instructions below. Sprinkle evenly with salt. Serve hot with creamy avocado salsa for dipping, optional.

OUTDOOR
Grill wings over medium-hot coals for 15-20 minutes, turning every 5 minutes, until the meat at the bone is opaque.

INDOOR
Preheat grill. Arrange the wings on a wire rack over an oven tray. Grill for 15-20 minutes, turning once, until the meat at the bone is opaque.

THINK AHEAD
Marinate the wings up to 8 hours in advance. Cover and refrigerate.

HONEY MUSTARD CHICKEN DRUMSTICKS

SERVES 4

6 garlic cloves, crushed	1 tsp black pepper
3 tbsp runny honey	8 drumsticks, slashed (see opposite)
2 tbsp creamy dijon mustard	salt
2 tbsp soy sauce	1 recipe roast garlic aïoli (see page
1 tbsp lemon juice	143), optional

Combine garlic, honey, mustard, soy sauce, lemon juice and pepper. Add drumsticks and toss to coat evenly. Cover and refrigerate for 1 hour. Grill according to instructions below. Sprinkle with salt. Serve hot with roast garlic aïoli for dipping, optional.

OUTDOOR
Grill over medium hot coals , turning every 3 minutes, until the chicken is opaque with no trace of pink at the bone, 15 minutes.

INDOOR
Preheat overhead grill. Grill, turning every 3 minutes, until the chicken is opaque with no trace of pink at the bone, 15 minutes.

THINK AHEAD
Marinate drumsticks up to 6 hours in advance. Cover and refrigerate.

SLASHING DRUMSTICKS
With sharp kitchen scissors, snip through skin to make deep cuts to the bone on both sides of the drumstick.

COOKS' NOTE
We slash drumsticks not only to allow flavouring to penetrate deeply, but to ensure that the meat is cooked through to the bone as quickly and evenly as possible.

SPICY TANDOORI CHICKEN DRUMSTICKS

SERVES 4

juice of 1 lemon
2 tsp black pepper
8 chicken drumsticks, slashed
  (see page 102)
2 garlic cloves, crushed
1 tbsp grated fresh ginger
3 tbsp spicy tandoori mix
  (see page 25)
150ml (5floz) Greek-style yoghurt
salt

Toss drumsticks with lemon juice and pepper. Cover and refrigerate for 30 minutes. Drain off lemon juice. Add garlic, ginger, tandoori mix and yoghurt to drumsticks. Toss to coat evenly. Cover and refrigerate for 1 hour. Shake off excess marinade and grill according to instructions below. Serve hot.

OUTDOOR
Grill over medium hot coals, turning every 3 minutes, until opaque with no trace of pink at the bone, 15 minutes.

INDOOR
Preheat overhead grill. Grill, turning every 3 minutes, until the chicken is opaque with no trace of pink at the bone, 15 minutes.

THINK AHEAD
Marinate drumsticks up to 6 hours in advance. Cover and refrigerate.

LEMON GINGER CHICKEN DRUMSTICKS WITH MANGO AND MUSTARD SEED GLAZE

SERVES 4

8 chicken drumsticks, slashed
  (see page 102)
FOR MARINADE
2 tbsp grated fresh ginger
2 garlic cloves, crushed
½ tsp chilli powder
juice of 1 lemon

FOR GLAZE
4 tbsp mango chutney, sieved
1 tbsp yellow mustard seeds
salt

For marinade, combine ginger, garlic, chilli powder and lemon juice. Add drumsticks and toss to coat evenly. Cover and refrigerate for 30 minutes. For glaze, combine chutney and mustard seeds. Grill according to instructions below, brushing with glaze throughout. Sprinkle with salt. Serve hot.

OUTDOOR
Grill over medium hot coals , turning every 3 minutes, until the chicken is opaque with no trace of pink at the bone, 15 minutes.

INDOOR
Preheat overhead grill. Grill, turning every 3 minutes, until the chicken is opaque with no trace of pink at the bone, 15 minutes.

THINK AHEAD
Marinate drumsticks up to 4 hours in advance. Cover and refrigerate, turning several times in marinade.

BONING CHICKEN LEG

Place leg skin side down. With a small, sharp knife, cut down the thigh towards the leg joint to expose the thigh bone. Lift the bone, scraping and making small cuts to release the flesh from the bone.

Hold the released thigh bone, and cut around joint to free. With the tip of the knife scrape down the length of the drumstick bone to expose, scraping and pushing the meat down and away from you. Stop scraping when you get to the knuckle end, at which stage you will have turned the chicken leg inside out.

With large chef's knife, cut off the bone about 2.5cm (1in) from the knuckle end. Reshape the chicken leg by turning skin right side out again.

THINK AHEAD
Bone chicken leg up to 1 day in advance. Cover tightly with cling film and refrigerate.

CHICKEN LEGS STUFFED WITH WILD MUSHROOMS

SERVES 4

4 chicken legs, boned (see opposite)
2 tsp salt
1 tsp black pepper

FOR STUFFING

1 tbsp olive oil
2 garlic cloves, crushed
4 shallots, finely chopped
1 tbsp fresh thyme leaves
200g (7oz) fresh wild mushrooms (see below), chopped
dash of brandy
1 tsp white truffle oil, optional
salt, black pepper

extra olive oil for brushing

ESSENTIAL EQUIPMENT

4 - 25cm (10in) presoaked bamboo skewers

Sprinkle salt and pepper inside chicken legs.

Heat oil in frying pan over high heat until hot but not smoking. Add garlic, shallots, thyme and mushrooms. Stir fry until wilted and starting to crisp, 5 minutes. Add brandy. Stand back from pan and set alight with a long match. Allow flames to burn out, then remove pan from heat and leave to cool completely. Stir in truffle oil if using and add salt and pepper to taste. Place boned chicken legs skin side down. Using a tablespoon, push a quarter of the mushroom mixture inside each leg cavity. Use the back of the spoon to spread some of this mushroom mixture up on to the inside of the thigh. Wrap the thigh meat around the stuffing and reshape. Pull the skin over to seal and thread skewer through the thigh to secure flaps. Grill according to instructions below. Serve hot.

OUTDOOR
Grill over medium-hot coals, basting regularly, until meat is opaque and stuffing is cooked through, 7-10 minutes per side.

THINK AHEAD
Stuff chicken legs up to 6 hours in advance. Remove from refrigerator and bring to room temperature before placing on the grill.

COOKS' NOTE
Make sure that the mushroom mixture is completely cool before stuffing. Placing a hot mixture into uncooked chicken could present a health hazard when done in advance.

A bunch of herbs makes an aromatic alternative to a basting brush. Choose robust, woody herbs such as thyme or rosemary.

INDOOR
Preheat oven to 200°C (400°F) gas 6. Brush chicken with olive oil and place on oven tray. Roast until cooked through, 20-25 minutes.

WILD MUSHROOMS
There are many varieties of wild mushrooms. Field or shiitake mushrooms are excellent for this recipe. Field mushrooms have an open, flat cap with exposed brown gills and a strong, savoury flavour. Shiitake mushrooms are a widely available oriental variety with a powerful meaty flavour. For a deluxe selection, choose from a mixture of chanterelles, cèpes (also called porcini) and morels.

To clean mushrooms, wipe clean with damp kitchen paper. Never wash or rinse mushrooms in water.

TARRAGON MUSTARD CHICKEN SKEWERS

SERVES 4

8 boneless, skinless chicken thighs
2 tbsp dried tarragon
4 tbsp creamy dijon mustard
4 tbsp red wine vinegar
2 tsp paprika
1 tbsp granulated sugar
1 tsp black pepper
salt
1 recipe creamy blue cheese sauce (see page 133), optional

ESSENTIAL EQUIPMENT
8 – 25cm (10 in) presoaked bamboo skewers

Cut each thigh into 6 equal-sized pieces. Thread pieces on to skewers. Combine tarragon, mustard, vinegar, paprika, sugar and pepper. Pour over skewered chicken. Cover and refrigerate for 30 minutes. Grill according to instructions below. Sprinkle with salt. Serve hot with creamy blue cheese sauce, optional.

OUTDOOR
Grill over medium-hot coals until the chicken is opaque with no trace of pink, 5 minutes per side.

INDOOR
Preheat overhead grill. Grill until the chicken is opaque with no trace of pink, 5 minutes per side.

THINK AHEAD
Marinate chicken up to 4 hours in advance. Cover and refrigerate.

CURRIED COCONUT CHICKEN

SERVES 4

8 boneless, skinless chicken thighs
4 garlic cloves, crushed
1 tbsp grated fresh ginger
1 onion, chopped
1 tbsp garam masala mix (see page 25)
1 handful fresh coriander
3 tbsp fish sauce
100ml (3½ floz) coconut milk
salt, black pepper
1 recipe oriental noodle salad (see page 150), optional

ESSENTIAL EQUIPMENT
16 – 25cm (10in) presoaked bamboo skewers

Spread chicken thighs flat. Thread 2 skewers diagonally through each thigh, to form a cross. Place garlic, ginger, onion, masala mix, coriander, fish sauce and coconut milk in a food processor or blender; pulse until smooth. Pour mixture over chicken. Cover and refrigerate for 30 minutes. Grill according to instructions below. Sprinkle with salt and pepper. Serve hot with oriental noodle salad, optional.

OUTDOOR
Grill over medium-hot coals until chicken is opaque with no trace of pink, 5 minutes per side.

INDOOR
Preheat overhead grill. Grill until chicken is opaque with no trace of pink, 5 minutes per side.

THINK AHEAD
Marinate chicken up to 6 hours in advance. Cover and refrigerate.

COOKS' NOTE
Skewering chicken thighs keeps them flat and open on the grill, allowing them to cook evenly.

GINGER HOISIN CHICKEN SKEWERS

SERVES 4

8 boneless, skinless chicken thighs
2 garlic cloves, chopped
3 tbsp grated fresh ginger
1 tbsp Chinese hot chilli sauce

1 tbsp soy sauce
1 tbsp dark brown sugar
4 tbsp hoisin sauce
8 spring onions, trimmed

ESSENTIAL EQUIPMENT
8 - 25cm (10in) presoaked bamboo skewers

Cut thighs into 2.5cm (1in) cubes. Combine garlic, ginger, chilli sauce, soy sauce, sugar and hoisin. Add chicken and toss to coat evenly. Cover and refrigerate for 30 minutes. Divide chicken cubes equally and skewer. Thread a spring onion over either end of each skewer, to form a bow shape round the chicken pieces. Grill according to instructions below. Serve hot.

OUTDOOR
Grill over medium-hot coals until chicken is opaque with no trace of pink, 5 minutes per side.

INDOOR
Preheat overhead grill. Grill until chicken is opaque with no trace of pink, 5 minutes per side.

THINK AHEAD
Marinate chicken up to 4 hours in advance. Cover and refrigerate.

CARDAMOM CHICKEN TIKKA

SERVES 4

8 boneless, skinless chicken thighs
juice of 1 lemon
2 tsp black pepper
1 tbsp grated fresh ginger
3 garlic cloves, crushed
1 tsp ground cardamom
½ tsp ground cumin
½ tsp ground nutmeg

1 fresh green chilli, seeded and
 finely chopped
1 tbsp double cream
3 tbsp Greek-style yoghurt
1½ lemons, cut into 8 wedges
salt
1 recipe cucumber yoghurt raita
 (see page 138), optional

ESSENTIAL EQUIPMENT
8 - 25cm (10in) presoaked bamboo skewers

Cut each thigh into 6 equal-sized pieces. Toss chicken pieces with lemon juice and
pepper. Cover and refrigerate for 30 minutes. Drain off lemon juice. Add ginger,
garlic, cardamom, cumin, nutmeg, chilli, cream and yoghurt to chicken. Toss together
to coat chicken well. Cover and refrigerate for 1 hour. Remove chicken cubes from
marinade, shaking off any excess. Thread on to skewers with lemon wedges.
Grill according to instructions below. Sprinkle with salt. Serve hot with cucumber
yoghurt raita, optional.

OUTDOOR
Grill over medium-hot coals until chicken is opaque
with no trace of pink, 5 minutes per side.

INDOOR
Preheat overhead grill. Grill until the chicken is
opaque with no trace of pink, 5 minutes per side.

THINK AHEAD
Marinate chicken up to 4 hours in advance. Cover and refrigerate.

COOKS' NOTE
It's best to grind the cardamom just before using, as its fragrance fades quickly after grinding. Lightly crush
the pods to remove the grain-like seeds, then crush (see page 161) until finely ground.

TERIYAKI CHICKEN

SERVES 4

4 tbsp shoyu (Japanese soy sauce)
2 tbsp mirin
4 tbsp sake
1 tbsp granulated sugar
8 boneless, skinless chicken thighs

ESSENTIAL EQUIPMENT
*8 attached pairs presoaked wooden chopsticks
or 8 - 25cm (10in) presoaked bamboo skewers*

Combine shoyu, mirin, sake and sugar in
small pan over medium heat. Bring to
the boil, stirring to dissolve the sugar.
Lower heat and simmer until thick and
syrupy, 5-10 minutes. Cool. Set aside
half the sauce for glazing the chicken.
Reserve remaining half to drizzle over
before serving. Cut each thigh into
3 even-sized pieces. Insert the blade of a
small, sharp knife through the middle of
each chicken piece to make a slit. Thread
3 slit pieces on to each pair of attached
chopsticks. Brush all over with the
cooled sauce to glaze. Grill according to
instructions below, basting with sauce.
Drizzle over reserved sauce. Serve hot.

OUTDOOR
Grill over medium hot
coals until the chicken is
opaque with no trace of
pink, 7 minutes per side.

INDOOR
Preheat overhead grill.
Grill until the chicken is
opaque with no trace of
pink, 7 minutes per side.

THINK AHEAD
Make sauce up to 3 days in advance. Cover and
refrigerate.

COOKS' NOTE
We like to serve teriyaki chicken on pairs of
chopsticks for a fun and impressive presentation.
Since they do not have sharpened ends, use a knife
to make an incision through the chicken to help you
slide the chicken pieces onto the chopsticks.
Alternatively, use presoaked bamboo skewers.

SPLITTING POULTRY

Place bird breast side down. With kitchen scissors or poultry shears, cut along each side of the backbone. Remove and discard.

Snip the wishbone and cut 1cm (½in) into the breast bone so that the bird can be pressed flat

THINK AHEAD
Split bird up to 1 day in advance. Cover tightly with cling film and refrigerate.

COOKS' NOTE
Splitting is a useful technique for the grill. Opening the birds flat and making them an equal thickness allows for quick, even cooking. The meat is cooked throughout without drying out.

We prefer to start cooking split birds bone side down as the heat of the grill takes longer to penetrate the denser, bony side. You can turn your attention to colouring the skin side nicely once you are sure that the bird is on its way to being cooked through.

LEMON PEPPERED POUSSIN

SERVES 4

4 poussin, split (see opposite)
1 lemon, peeled and chopped
  (see page 161)
2 tsp crushed chilli flakes
2 garlic cloves, crushed

2 tbsp worcestershire sauce
4 tbsp sunflower oil
salt, black pepper
1 recipe roast garlic aïoli
  (see page 143), optional

ESSENTIAL EQUIPMENT
8 - 35cm (14in) flat metal skewers

Place a poussin cut side down and press flat. Push a skewer horizontally through the wings and breast. Push another skewer horizontally through the thighs. Repeat with remaining poussin and skewers.
Combine lemon, chilli flakes, garlic, worcestershire sauce and oil in a large dish. Add poussin, turning to coat both sides. Cover and refrigerate for 30 minutes. Grill according to instructions below. Remove skewers. Sprinkle with salt and pepper. Serve hot with roast garlic aïoli, optional.

OUTDOOR
Grill bone side down over medium-hot coals for 15 minutes. Turn and grill skin side down until skin is crispy and there is no trace of pink at the bone, 10 minutes.

INDOOR
Preheat overhead grill. Grill bone side up for 15 minutes. Turn and grill skin side up until skin is crispy and there is no trace of pink at the bone, 10 minutes.

THINK AHEAD
Marinate poussin up to 3 hours in advance. Cover and refrigerate, turning several times.

SPLIT POUSSIN VARIATION
SPICY JERK POUSSIN

Replace lemon, chilli flakes, garlic, worcestershire sauce and oil with spicy jerk rub (see page 24). Omit roast garlic aïoli when serving.

SCORING DUCK SKIN

With a sharp knife, cut diagonal parallel slashes 1cm (½in) apart through skin to make diamond pattern. Be careful not to pierce the flesh.

COOKS' NOTE
Scoring is essential if you want perfectly crisp duck. The scored surface allows the layer of fat under the skin to melt away so that the outer skin can crisp.

CRISPY BALSAMIC DUCK

SERVES 4

5 tbsp balsamic vinegar
4 duck breasts, scored (see opposite)
salt, black pepper
1 tbsp extra balsamic vinegar for drizzling

Put 5 tbsp vinegar in a shallow dish just wide enough to fit 4 breasts. Add the duck breasts, skin side up. Cover and leave to marinate for 20 minutes at room temperature. Grill or roast according to instructions below. Cover with foil and leave to rest for 5 minutes before cutting into thin slices (see below). Sprinkle with salt and pepper. Drizzle over remaining balsamic vinegar. Serve hot.

OUTDOOR
Grill over medium coals, skin side down until the skin is crispy, 5 minutes. Turn and grill for further 8 minutes for medium rare, 10 minutes for well-done.

INDOOR
Preheat oven to 200°C (400°F) gas 6. Preheat a heavy oven-proof pan over medium heat. Add duck skin side down and cook until crispy, 5 minutes. Turn breasts and place pan in the oven for 8 minutes for medium rare, 10 minutes for well done.

THINK AHEAD
Marinate duck breasts up to 2 hours in advance. Cover and refrigerate.

COOKS' NOTE
We like to serve this tangy duck dish with a slice of roasted onion focaccia with rosemary (see page 155).

SPICED SOY DUCK

SERVES 4

2 tbsp runny honey
1 tbsp soy sauce
½ tsp Chinese five-spice powder
4 duck breasts, scored (see page 111)

Combine honey, soy sauce and spice. Put mixture in a shallow dish just wide enough to fit 4 breasts. Add the duck breasts, skin side up. Cover and leave to marinate for 20 minutes at room temperature. Grill or roast according to instructions below. Cover with foil and leave to rest for 5 minutes before slicing across on the diagonal. Serve hot.

OUTDOOR
Grill over medium coals, skin side down until the skin is crispy, 5 minutes. Turn and grill for a further 8 minutes for medium rare, 10 minutes for well done.

INDOOR
Preheat oven to 200°C (400°F) gas 6. Preheat a heavy oven-proof pan over medium heat. Add duck skin side down and cook until crispy, 5 minutes. Turn breasts and place pan in the oven for 8 minutes for medium rare, 10 minutes for well done.

THINK AHEAD
Marinate duck breasts up to 2 hours in advance. Cover and refrigerate.

COOKS' NOTE
Fresh papaya sambal (see page 137) and sesame soba noodle salad (see page 148) are both delicious accompaniments to this spicy duck.

DUCK WITH SWEET ORANGE GLAZE

SERVES 4

juice of 2 oranges
2 tbsp runny honey
4 duck breasts, scored (see page 111)
salt, black pepper

For glaze, combine 2 tbsp of the orange juice with honey. Put remaining orange juice in a shallow dish just wide enough for 4 breasts. Add the duck breasts, skin side up. Cover and leave to marinate for 20 minutes at room temperature. Grill or roast according to instructions below, basting with glaze throughout. Cover with foil and leave to rest for 5 minutes before cutting on the diagonal into thin slices. Sprinkle with salt and pepper. Serve hot.

OUTDOOR
Grill over medium coals, skin side down until the skin is crispy, 5 minutes. Turn and grill for further 8 minutes for medium rare, 10 minutes for well done.

INDOOR
Preheat oven to 200°C (400°F) gas 6. Preheat a heavy oven-proof pan over medium heat. Add duck skin side down and cook until crispy, 5 minutes. Turn breasts and place pan in the oven for 8 minutes for medium rare, 10 minutes for well done.

THINK AHEAD
Marinate duck breasts up to 2 hours in advance. Cover and refrigerate.

COOKS' NOTE
A crisp, green leaf salad with honey mustard dressing (see page 152) is the perfect match for this succulent, savoury duck.

CINNAMON QUAIL WITH POMEGRANATE GLAZE

SERVES 4

8 quail, split (see page 110)
1 tsp ground cinnamon
2 tbsp pomegranate molasses
1 tbsp olive oil
salt, black pepper

ESSENTIAL EQUIPMENT
8 - 35cm (14in) flat metal skewers

Place 2 quail cut side down and press flat. Push a skewer horizontally through the wings and breast of both quail. Push another skewer horizontally through the thighs. Repeat with remaining quail and skewers. Combine cinnamon and pomegranate molasses and rub over quail. Cover with cling film and refrigerate for 30 minutes. Remove from refrigerator and bring to room temperature. Drizzle over oil. Grill according to instructions below. Sprinkle with salt and pepper. Serve hot.

OUTDOOR
Grill bone side down over medium-hot coals for 8 minutes. Turn and grill skin side down, until the meat is opaque and there is no trace of pink at the bone, a further 5 minutes.

INDOOR
Preheat overhead grill. Grill bone side up for 8 minutes. Turn and grill skin side up until skin is crispy and there is no trace of pink at the bone, a further 5 minutes.

THINK AHEAD
Marinate quail up to 4 hours in advance. Cover and refrigerate.

COOKS' NOTE
Pomegranate molasses - also referred to as syrup and concentrate - is made by boiling down pomegranate juice to a thick dark brown liquid with a distinctive sweet sour flavour. It's a favourite flavouring across the Middle East but especially in Iran, Syria and Lebanon. Look for it in Middle-Eastern shops or order it from a gourmet mail order company (see page 167). Alternatively, use date molasses, which is available in health food stores.

ROSEMARY GARLIC QUAIL

SERVES 4

8 quail, split (see page 110)
1 tsp dried rosemary
2 garlic cloves, crushed
½ tsp black pepper
¼ tsp crushed chilli flakes
1 tbsp lemon juice
1 tbsp olive oil

ESSENTIAL EQUIPMENT
8 - 35cm (14in) flat metal skewers

Place 2 quail cut side down and press flat. Push a skewer horizontally through the wings and breast of both quail. Push another skewer horizontally through the thighs. Repeat with remaining quail and skewers. Combine rosemary, garlic, pepper, chilli flakes, lemon juice and oil. Leave mixture to stand at room temperature for 30 minutes to allow flavours to combine. Brush mixture over quail. Grill according to instructions below, basting throughout with remaining mixture. Sprinkle with salt. Serve hot.

OUTDOOR
Grill bone side down over medium-hot coals for 8 minutes. Turn and grill skin side down, until the meat is opaque and there is no trace of pink at the bone, a further 5 minutes.

INDOOR
Preheat overhead grill. Grill bone side up for 8 minutes. Turn and grill skin side up until skin is crispy and there is no trace of pink at the bone, a further 5 minutes.

THINK AHEAD
Make marinade up to 1 day in advance. Cover and store at room temperature.

COOKS' NOTE
The intense, sun-filled flavours of slow roast tomato salad (see page 147) perfectly complement these grilled Tuscan-style quails. This aromatic and spicy marinade is also delicious with split poussin (see page 110 for cooking times).

VEGETABLES ON THE GRILL

CHARGRILLED BALSAMIC RED ONIONS

SERVES 4
2 large red onions
2 tbsp olive oil
1 tbsp balsamic vinegar
salt, black pepper
1 tbsp each extra olive oil and balsamic vinegar to drizzle
1 tsp fresh thyme leaves

ESSENTIAL EQUIPMENT
4 – 35cm (14in) flat metal skewers

Trim off and discard the root and stalk ends of the onions. Cut each onion into 1.5cm (⅜in) rounds. Thread rounds on to skewers. Brush both sides of each skewered round with oil. Sprinkle with balsamic vinegar, salt and pepper. Grill according to instructions below. Drizzle over remaining oil and vinegar. Sprinkle with thyme. Serve hot.

OUTDOOR
Grill over medium coals until tender and lightly charred, 5 minutes per side.

INDOOR
Preheat overhead grill. Grill until lightly charred, 5 minutes per side.

CHAR-ROAST ROSEMARY ONIONS

SERVES 4
4 unpeeled large yellow or red onions
2 tbsp red wine or sherry vinegar
2 tbsp olive oil
salt, black pepper
1 tsp finely chopped fresh rosemary
2 tbsp olive oil to drizzle
¹/₂ tbsp fresh rosemary leaves

Preheat oven to 180°C (350°F) gas 4.
Cut onions in half from top to bottom. Trim and peel each onion half, leaving the root end attached to allow the onion halves to stay intact when cooking. Arrange onion halves on an oven tray, cut side up. Sprinkle evenly with vinegar, oil, salt, pepper and chopped rosemary. Cover with foil and pre-roast for 30 minutes. Grill according to instructions below. Drizzle with olive oil and sprinkle with rosemary leaves. Serve hot.

OUTDOOR
Grill over medium-hot coals until lightly charred, 5 minutes per side.

INDOOR
Preheat overhead grill. Grill until lightly charred, 5 minutes per side.

THINK AHEAD
Pre-roast onions in oven up to 1 day in advance. Cover and store at room temperature.

COOKS' NOTE
These onions make a great vegetarian main course when served with creamy blue cheese sauce (see page 133).

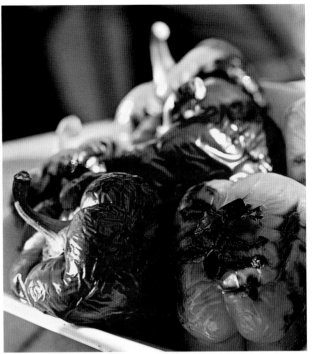

CHARGRILLED CORN ON THE COB WITH CORIANDER CHILLI BUTTER

SERVES 4

4 ears fresh sweetcorn
2 tbsp melted butter
salt, black pepper
4 - 1.5cm (¾ in) slices coriander chilli butter
 (see page 140)
lime wedges

Cook corn in unsalted boiling water for 2 minutes. Refresh in cold water. Brush with melted butter. Grill according to instructions below. Sprinkle with salt and pepper. Serve each ear hot with a slice of coriander chilli butter and a wedge of lime.

OUTDOOR
Grill over medium-hot coals, turning frequently, until lightly charred, 5 minutes.

INDOOR
Preheat overhead grill. Grill, turning frequently until lightly charred, 5 minutes.

THINK AHEAD
Boil corn up to 1 day in advance. Refresh immediately in cold water. Cover and refrigerate. Grill just before serving.

COOKS' NOTE
We also love chargrilled corn on the cob spread with roast garlic aïoli (see page 143).

CHAR-ROAST PEPPERS

SERVES 4

3 red, yellow or orange peppers
1 tbsp balsamic vinegar
3 tbsp olive oil
salt, black pepper

Grill peppers whole according to instructions below. Place grilled peppers in a plastic bag or a bowl with a plate on top. Leave for 5-10 minutes until cool enough to handle. Uncover and peel off charred skin. Discard stems and seeds (see page 160). Slice peppers into 1cm (½ in) wide strips. Toss strips with vinegar and oil. Add salt and pepper to taste. Serve warm or at room temperature.

OUTDOOR
Grill over flaming coals, turning frequently, until skin is charred all over, 10 minutes.

INDOOR
Preheat overhead grill. Place under grill, turning frequently, until skin is charred all over, 10 minutes.

THINK AHEAD
Grill peppers up to 1 day in advance. Store covered at room temperature.

CHARGRILLED NEW POTATO SKEWERS

SERVES 4

750g (1½ lb) unpeeled new potatoes
3 tbsp olive oil
salt, black pepper

ESSENTIAL EQUIPMENT

4 - 25cm (10in) presoaked bamboo skewers

Cook potatoes in boiling salted water until just tender,
15 minutes. Cut in half and toss with oil, salt and pepper.
Thread potato halves on to skewers. Grill according to
instructions below. Serve hot.

OUTDOOR
Grill over medium coals, turning
regularly, until lightly charred, 10
minutes.

INDOOR
Preheat overhead grill. Grill, turning
regularly, until lightly charred,
10 minutes.

THINK AHEAD
Pre-cook potatoes up to 1 day in advance. Cut in half, toss in oil and skewer up
to 2 hours in advance. Cover and keep at room temperature until ready to grill.

CHARGRILLED TOMATOES

SERVES 4

4 ripe tomatoes, halved
1 tbsp olive oil
salt, black pepper

Place tomato halves skin side down. Sprinkle with oil, salt and
pepper. Grill according to instructions below. Serve hot or at
room temperature.

OUTDOOR
Grill over medium-hot coals until lightly
charred on the outside but still firm,
3 minutes per side.

INDOOR
Preheat overhead grill. Grill until lightly
charred on the outside but still firm,
3 minutes per side.

CHARGRILLED GARLIC POTATO SLICES

SERVES 4

750g (1½ lb) unpeeled plain or sweet potatoes, sliced
  1cm (½ in) thick
2 garlic cloves, crushed
4 tbsp olive oil
salt, black pepper
1 recipe roast garlic aïoli (see page 143), optional

Cook potato slices in boiling salted water until tender but still
firm, 5 minutes. Drain. Combine the garlic and oil. Brush potato
slices with garlic oil. Grill according to instructions below.
Sprinkle with salt and pepper. Serve hot with aïoli, optional.

OUTDOOR
Grill over medium coals until lightly
charred, 5 minutes per side.

INDOOR
Preheat overhead grill. Grill until lightly
charred, 5 minutes per side.

THINK AHEAD
Boil potato slices up to 4 hours in advance. Cool, cover and keep at room
temperature until ready to grill.

CHARGRILLED AUBERGINE SLICES WITH LEMON TAHINI SAUCE

SERVES 4

2 aubergines cut into 1cm (¹/₂ in) thick slices
8 tbsp olive oil
salt, black pepper
1 recipe lemon tahini sauce (see page 132)

Brush the aubergine slices on both sides with olive oil. Grill according to instructions below. Sprinkle with salt and pepper. Serve hot or at room temperature with lemon tahini sauce.

OUTDOOR
Grill over medium-hot coals until lightly charred and tender, 5 minutes per side.

INDOOR
Preheat a ridged cast iron grill pan over high heat. Grill until lightly charred and tender, 5 minutes per side.

THINK AHEAD
Grill aubergines up to 6 hours in advance. Cover and store at room temperature.

COOKS' NOTE
Salsa verde (see page 134), charmoula (see page 23), spicy peanut sauce (see page 136), roast pepper and basil salsa (see page 138) or spiced chickpea sauce (see page 137) are all excellent choices to serve with these aubergine slices in place of the lemon tahini sauce.

CHAR-ROAST AUBERGINE WITH SESAME AND HONEY MISO GLAZE

SERVES 4

4 tbsp honey miso sauce (see page 138)
2 tbsp sesame seeds
2 aubergines
extra honey miso sauce for drizzling

For glaze, combine honey miso sauce and sesame seeds. Prick aubergines all over with fork. Grill according to instructions below. Cut in half lengthwise. Score a crisscross pattern 1cm (½ in) deep into the aubergine flesh. Brush scored side with glaze. Grill glazed cut side down until sizzling and tender, a further 5 minutes. Serve hot with extra honey miso sauce drizzled over.

OUTDOOR
Grill over medium coals, turning frequently until charred all over, 15 minutes. Leave until cool enough to handle, about 10 minutes.

INDOOR
Preheat overhead grill. Grill, turning frequently, until charred all over, 15 minutes. Leave until cool enough to handle, about 10 minutes.

AUBERGINE VARIATION

CHAR-ROAST AUBERGINE WITH SPICY PEANUT SAUCE

SERVES 4

Omit honey miso sauce and sesame seeds. Spread scored side of aubergines with 4 tbsp spicy peanut sauce (see page 136). Serve with remaining spicy peanut sauce.

CHARGRILLED COURGETTES WITH ROAST PEPPER AND BASIL SALSA

SERVES 4

500g (1lb) courgettes, sliced 1cm (½in) thick lengthwise
3 tbsp olive oil
salt, black pepper
1 recipe roast pepper and basil salsa (see page 138)

Grill courgettes according to instructions below. Arrange on platter. Spoon over salsa and serve hot or at room temperature.

OUTDOOR
Grill over medium coals until lightly charred and tender, 5 -10 minutes per side.

INDOOR
Preheat a ridged cast iron grill pan over high heat. Grill until lightly charred and tender, 5-10 minutes per side.

COOKS' NOTE
This makes a great vegetarian main course when served with radish tzatziki (see page 135) or creamy blue cheese sauce (see page 133).

CHARGRILLED SQUASH WITH JERKED HONEY RUM GLAZE

SERVES 4

500g (1lb) unpeeled butternut squash, cut into
1cm (½in) thick slices
1 recipe jerked honey rum glaze (see page 25)
salt, black pepper

Bring a large pan of water to the boil. Add squash slices and when water returns to rolling boil, drain. Arrange in a single layer on a tea towel and pat dry. Grill according to instructions below. Sprinkle with salt and pepper and serve hot.

OUTDOOR
Grill over medium-hot coals, brushing with glaze and turning once until lightly charred, 3 minutes per side.

INDOOR
Preheat overhead grill. Brush with glaze and grill until browned, 3 minutes per side.

THINK AHEAD
Pre-cook squash up to 4 hours in advance. Cover and leave at room temperature until ready to grill.

CHARGRILLED NECTARINES

SERVES 4

4 nectarines, halved and stoned
1 tbsp runny honey
vanilla ice cream

Brush cut sides of nectarine halves with honey. Grill according to instructions below. Serve hot with a scoop of vanilla ice cream.

OUTDOOR
Grill cut side down over medium-low coals until warm and lightly charred, but still firm, 5 minutes.

INDOOR
Preheat overhead grill. Grill cut side up until warm and lightly charred, but still firm, 5 minutes.

CHARGRILLED PINEAPPLE WITH SWEET RUM GLAZE

SERVES 4

1 unpeeled medium pineapple, quartered
2 tbsp dark rum
1 tbsp lime juice
2 tbsp honey

Cut away the core from the pineapple quarters. For glaze, combine rum, lime juice and honey and stir to dissolve. Grill according to instructions below. Serve hot with any remaining glaze drizzled over.

OUTDOOR
Grill over medium-low coals, brushing with glaze, until hot and lightly charred, 5-10 minutes per side.

INDOOR
Preheat overhead grill. Brush with glaze and grill until hot and lightly charred, 5-10 minutes per side.

VARIATION
CHARGRILLED PINEAPPLE WITH JERKED HONEY RUM GLAZE

Replace sweet rum glaze with jerked honey rum glaze (see page 25).

GRILL ROAST CINNAMON RUM BANANAS

SERVES 4

**4 large bananas, cut on diagonal into
  2.5cm (1in) thick slices
juice of 1 lime
1 tbsp dark brown sugar
2 tbsp dark rum
1 tsp ground cinnamon
vanilla ice cream**

ESSENTIAL EQUIPMENT
4 - 30cm (12in) squares of extra thick or heavy duty foil

Toss banana slices with lime juice, sugar, rum and cinnamon. Divide bananas among foil squares. Bring the edges of foil together and scrunch to seal. Grill roast according to instructions below. Serve warm with a scoop of vanilla ice cream.

OUTDOOR
Grill over medium-low coals until hot through, 15-20 minutes.

INDOOR
Preheat oven to 200°C (400°F) gas 6. Bake until hot through, 10-15 minutes.

THINK AHEAD
Assemble foil packets up to 1 hour in advance. Store at room temperature.

GRILL ROAST LEMON LIQUEUR STRAWBERRIES

SERVES 4

**500g (1lb) strawberries, hulled and halved
3 tbsp Grand Marnier
grated zest of 1 lemon
2 tbsp granulated sugar
vanilla ice cream**

ESSENTIAL EQUIPMENT
4 - 30cm (12in) squares of extra thick or heavy duty foil

Toss strawberry halves with Grand Marnier, lemon zest and sugar. Divide strawberries among foil squares. Bring the edges of foil together and scrunch to seal. Grill roast according to instructions below. Serve warm with a scoop of vanilla ice cream.

OUTDOOR
Grill over medium-low coals until warm through, 5-10 minutes.

INDOOR
Preheat oven to 200°C (400°F) gas 6. Bake until warm through, 5 minutes.

THINK AHEAD
Assemble foil packets up to 1 hour in advance. Store at room temperature.

GRILL ROAST SWEET SPICED ORANGES

SERVES 4

**4 oranges, peeled (see page 161) and cut into
  2.5cm (1in) slices
1½ tbsp dark brown sugar
2 tsp brandy
1 tsp cardamom pods**

ESSENTIAL EQUIPMENT
4 - 30cm (12in) squares of extra thick or heavy duty foil

Toss orange slices with sugar and brandy. Divide orange slices among foil squares. Sprinkle with cardamom pods. Bring the edges of foil together and scrunch to seal. Grill roast according to instructions below. Serve hot.

OUTDOOR
Grill over medium-low coals until hot through, 15-20 minutes.

INDOOR
Preheat oven to 200°C (400°F) gas 6. Bake until hot through, 10-15 minutes.

THINK AHEAD
Assemble foil packets up to 2 hours in advance. Store at room temperature.

GRILL ROAST HONEY ORANGE FIGS

SERVES 4

**8 figs, halved
4 tbsp runny honey
juice of 1 orange
grated zest of 1 orange
4 tbsp mascarpone or crème fraîche**

ESSENTIAL EQUIPMENT
4 - 30cm (12in) squares of extra thick or heavy duty foil

Divide fig halves cut side up among foil squares. Drizzle over honey and orange juice and sprinkle with zest. Bring the edges of foil together and scrunch to seal. Grill roast according to instructions below. Serve hot with mascarpone or crème fraîche.

OUTDOOR
Grill over medium-low coals until hot through, 15-20 minutes.

INDOOR
Preheat oven to 200°C (400°F) gas 6. Bake until hot through, 10-15 minutes.

THINK AHEAD
Assemble foil packets up to 2 hours in advance. Store at room temperature.

CHARGRILLED QUESADILLAS WITH SPICY CORIANDER

SERVES 4

1 handful fresh coriander
2 garlic cloves, crushed
1 green chilli, seeded and finely chopped
4 spring onions, chopped
½ tsp ground coriander
½ tsp ground cumin
2 tbsp lime juice
8 tbsp olive oil
salt, black pepper
8 - 20cm (8in) flour tortillas
200g (7oz) gruyère cheese, grated
1 recipe avocado mango salsa (see page 136)
150ml (5floz) sour cream, optional

Place fresh coriander, garlic, chilli, spring onion, ground coriander, cumin, lime juice and oil in a food processor or blender; pulse to a smooth paste. Add salt and pepper to taste. Spread a quarter of the coriander paste over 1 tortilla. Top evenly with a quarter of the cheese. Lightly press a second tortilla on top. Repeat with remaining tortillas, salsa and cheese. Grill according to instructions below. Cut into wedges with kitchen scissors or a sharp serrated knife. Serve hot with avocado mango salsa and sour cream, optional, spooned over each wedge.

OUTDOOR
Grill over medium-hot coals until lightly charred and the cheese is melted, 2 minutes per side.

INDOOR
Preheat a ridged cast iron grill pan over high heat. Grill until lightly charred and the cheese is melted, 2 minutes per side.

THINK AHEAD
Assemble tortillas up to 4 hours in advance. Cover with cling film and leave at room temperature until ready to grill.

CHARGRILLED QUESADILLAS WITH SALSA FRESCA

SERVES 4

8 - 20cm (8in) flour tortillas
100g (3½oz) gruyère cheese, grated
1 recipe salsa fresca (see page 133)
200g (7oz) feta cheese, crumbled
1 recipe creamy avocado salsa (see page 132), optional

Spread a quarter of the gruyère over 1 tortilla. Top evenly with a quarter of the salsa fresca. Sprinkle with a quarter of the feta. Lightly press a second tortilla on top. Repeat with remaining tortillas, gruyère, salsa and feta. Grill according to instructions below. Cut into wedges with kitchen scissors or a sharp serrated knife. Serve hot with creamy avocado salsa spooned over each wedge, if desired.

OUTDOOR
Grill over medium-hot coals until lightly charred and the gruyère is melted, 2 minutes per side.

INDOOR
Preheat a ridged cast iron grill pan over high heat. Grill until lightly charred and the gruyère is melted, 2 minutes per side.

THINK AHEAD
Assemble tortillas up to 4 hours in advance. Cover with cling film and leave at room temperature until ready to grill.

CHARGRILLED AUBERGINE, GOAT'S CHEESE AND MINT BRUSCHETTA

SERVES 4

8 slices day old ciabatta or country-style bread, 1cm (½in) thick
1 medium aubergine, cut crosswise into 1cm (½in) thick slices
4 tbsp olive oil for brushing

FOR DRESSING
1 tbsp finely chopped fresh mint
1 tbsp balsamic vinegar
1 tbsp olive oil
salt, black pepper

8 tbsp fresh creamy goat's cheese
extra olive oil for drizzling

Toast bread slices until crisp, about 2 minutes per side.
Brush the aubergine slices on both sides with olive oil. Grill according to instructions below. Toss aubergine slices gently with mint, vinegar and oil. Sprinkle with salt and pepper to taste. Spread bruschetta with equal amounts of goat's cheese. Top with aubergine and drizzle with extra olive oil. Serve at room temperature.

OUTDOOR
Grill over medium-hot coals until lightly charred and tender, 5 minutes per side.

INDOOR
Preheat a ridged cast iron grill pan over high heat. Grill until lightly charred and tender, 5 minutes per side.

THINK AHEAD
Toast bruschetta up to 1 day in advance. Store in an airtight container at room temperature. Grill aubergine up to 6 hours in advance. Leave covered at room temperature until ready to serve.

CHAR-ROAST LEMON OREGANO PEPPERS ON BRUSCHETTA

SERVES 4

8 slices of day old ciabatta or country-style bread, 1cm (½in) thick
3 red peppers
2 tbsp lemon juice

2 garlic cloves, crushed
2 tsp finely chopped fresh oregano
5 tbsp olive oil
salt, black pepper

Toast bread slices until crisp, 2 minutes per side.
Grill peppers according to instructions below. Place grilled peppers in a plastic bag or a bowl with a plate on top. Leave for 5-10 minutes until cool enough to handle. Uncover and peel off charred skin (see page 160). Discard stems and seeds (see page 160). Slice peppers into 1cm (½in) wide strips. Toss strips with lemon, garlic, oregano and oil. Add salt and pepper to taste. Top bruschetta with equal amounts of dressed peppers. Serve warm or at room temperature.

OUTDOOR
Grill over flaming coals, turning frequently, until skin is charred all over, 10 minutes.

INDOOR
Preheat overhead grill. Place under grill, turning frequently, until skin is charred all over, 10 minutes.

THINK AHEAD
Prepare bruschetta and peppers up to one day in advance. Store bruschetta in an airtight container at room temperature. Store peppers separately at room temperature.

Sauces & Salsas

CREAMY AVOCADO SALSA

MAKES 500ml (16floz)

2 avocados, halved and stoned
6 spring onions, chopped
1 handful fresh coriander
2 tbsp red wine vinegar
2 tbsp olive oil
250ml (8floz) sour cream
salt, black pepper

Place avocado, spring onion, coriander, vinegar, oil and sour cream in a food processor or blender; pulse to a smooth purée. Add salt and pepper to taste. Cover and refrigerate for 30 minutes to allow flavours to blend. Serve chilled.

THINK AHEAD
Make salsa up to 1 day in advance. Cover and refrigerate.

COOKS' NOTE
To prevent discoloration, store in a bowl with cling film, pressing directly on the salsa to prevent contact with air.

LEMON TAHINI SAUCE

MAKES 250ml (8floz)

100ml (3½ floz) tahini
1 garlic clove, crushed
juice of 1 lemon
125ml (4floz) water
salt, black pepper

Whisk tahini, garlic and lemon juice together until smooth. Whisk in water. Add salt and pepper to taste. Cover and let stand at room temperature for 30 minutes to allow flavours to blend. Serve chilled or at room temperature.

THINK AHEAD
Make sauce up to 2 days in advance. Cover and refrigerate.

CREAMY BLUE CHEESE SAUCE

MAKES 500ml (16floz)

6 spring onions, chopped
200g (7oz) blue cheese
300ml (10floz) sour cream
1 tsp worcestershire sauce
salt, black pepper

Place spring onion, cheese, cream and worcestershire sauce in a food processor or blender; pulse until smooth. Add salt and pepper to taste. Cover and refrigerate for 30 minutes to allow flavours to blend. Serve chilled.

THINK AHEAD
Make sauce up to 1 day in advance. Cover and refrigerate. Leave to stand at room temperature for 15 minutes to soften slightly before serving.

SALSA FRESCA

MAKES ABOUT 375ml (13floz)

6 medium tomatoes, seeded (see page 161)
  and finely diced
1 red onion, finely chopped
2 garlic cloves, crushed
1 fresh green chilli, seeded and finely chopped
1 tbsp lime juice
2 tbsp olive oil
2 tbsp finely chopped fresh coriander
salt, black pepper

Combine tomatoes, onion, garlic, chilli, lime juice, oil and coriander. Add salt and pepper to taste. Cover and let stand for 30 minutes at room temperature to allow flavours to blend. Serve chilled or at room temperature.

THINK AHEAD
Make salsa up to 1 day in advance. Cover and refrigerate.

SALSA VERDE

MAKES 175ml (6floz)

2 handfuls flat-leaf parsley
10 fresh basil leaves
10 fresh mint leaves
1 garlic clove, crushed
1 tbsp creamy dijon mustard
1 tbsp drained capers
2 anchovy fillets
½ tsp red wine vinegar
150ml (5floz) olive oil
salt, black pepper

Place parsley, basil, mint, garlic,
mustard, capers, anchovy, vinegar and
oil in a food processor or blender; pulse
to a purée. Add salt and pepper to taste.
Cover and let stand for 30 minutes at
room temperature to allow flavours to
blend. Serve at room temperature.

THINK AHEAD
Make salsa up to 3 days in advance. Cover and refrigerate.
Bring to room temperature and stir before serving.

PINEAPPLE LIME SALSA

MAKES 375ml (13floz)

½ fresh pineapple, cored
 and finely diced
1 fresh red chilli, seeded
 and finely chopped
1 red onion, finely chopped
2 tbsp finely chopped fresh
 coriander or mint
grated zest 1 lime
3 tbsp lime juice
salt, tabasco

Combine pineapple, chilli, onion,
coriander or mint, lime zest and lime juice.
Add salt and tabasco to taste. Cover and
let stand for 30 minutes at room
temperature to allow flavours to blend.
Serve chilled or at room temperature.

THINK AHEAD
Make salsa up to 3 hours in advance. Cover and
refrigerate.

COOKS' NOTE
A serrated knife is the best tool for cutting away the
peel from a fresh pineapple. Cut off the leaves at
their base and the bottom rind first. Stand the
pineapple on its base and cut off the rind from the
sides, using downward strokes.

RADISH TZATZIKI

MAKES 500ml (16floz)

150g (5oz) radishes, grated
1 red onion, grated
2 garlic cloves, crushed
1 tbsp red wine vinegar
1 tsp granulated sugar
175ml (6floz) Greek-style yoghurt
salt, black pepper

Combine radishes, onion, garlic, vinegar, sugar and yoghurt. Add salt and pepper to taste. Cover and refrigerate for 30 minutes to allow flavours to blend. Serve chilled.

THINK AHEAD
Make tzatziki up to 1 day in advance. Cover and refrigerate. Stir before serving.

CHIMI CHURRI

MAKES 175ml (6floz)

2 handfuls flat-leaf parsley leaves
4 spring onions, chopped
8 garlic cloves, crushed
1 tsp dried oregano
½ tsp crushed chilli flakes
4 tbsp red wine vinegar
8 tbsp sunflower oil
salt, black pepper

Place parsley, spring onion, garlic, oregano, chilli flakes, vinegar and oil in a food processor or blender; pulse until well blended but still retaining some texture. Add salt and pepper to taste. Cover and let stand for 30 minutes at room temperature to allow flavours to blend. Serve chilled or at room temperature.

THINK AHEAD
Make up to 3 days in advance, but add the vinegar just 2 hours before serving.

COOKS' NOTE
When making this colourful sauce more than a couple of hours in advance, be sure to follow the instructions for adding vinegar at a later time. If added too far in advance, the vinegar will "cook" the parsley, causing the vibrant green colour of the sauce to fade.

AVOCADO MANGO SALSA

MAKES 375ml (13floz)

1 mango, finely diced
1 avocado, halved, stoned and finely diced
½ red onion, finely chopped
1 red chilli, seeded and finely chopped
1 tbsp lime juice
1 tbsp red wine vinegar
2 tbsp olive oil
2 tbsp finely chopped mint
salt, tabasco

Combine mango, avocado, onion, chilli, lime juice, vinegar, oil
and mint. Add salt and tabasco to taste. Cover and let stand
for 30 minutes at room temperature to allow flavours to blend.
Serve chilled or at room temperature.

THINK AHEAD
Make salsa up to 6 hours before serving. Cover and refrigerate.

COOKS' NOTE
To prevent discoloration, store in a bowl with cling film, pressing directly on the
salsa to prevent contact with air.

SPICY PEANUT SAUCE

MAKES 500ml (16floz)

250g (8oz) peanut butter
2 garlic cloves, crushed
1 tbsp grated fresh ginger
1 tsp turmeric
1 tsp tabasco
1 tbsp toasted sesame oil
4 tbsp soy sauce
2 tbsp runny honey
juice of 1 lemon
125ml (4floz) water

Place peanut butter, garlic, ginger, turmeric, tabasco, oil, soy
sauce, honey, lemon juice and water in a food processor or
blender; pulse until smooth. Cover and let stand for 30 minutes
at room temperature to allow flavours to blend. Serve chilled
or at room temperature.

THINK AHEAD
Make sauce up to 3 days in advance. Cover and refrigerate.

COOKS' NOTE
For a spicy peanut dip with an extra-rich coconut flavour, replace the water with
an equal amount of coconut milk.

FRESH PAPAYA SAMBAL

MAKES ABOUT 250ml (8floz)

1 papaya, seeded and finely chopped
½ red onion, finely chopped
1 tbsp finely chopped coriander
2 tbsp lime juice
1 tbsp fish sauce
1 tsp sugar
salt, black pepper

Combine papaya, onion, coriander, lime juice, fish sauce and
sugar. Add salt and pepper to taste. Cover and let stand for
30 minutes at room temperature to allow flavours to blend.
Serve chilled or at room temperature.

THINK AHEAD
Make sambal up to 4 hours in advance. Cover and refrigerate. Stir before serving.

COOKS' NOTE
This recipe is also delicious when mango is used in place of the papaya.

SPICED CHICKPEA SAUCE

MAKES 500ml (16floz)

1 - 400g (14oz) tin chickpeas, drained and rinsed
2 garlic cloves, crushed
½ tsp ground cumin
¼ tsp tabasco
2 tbsp lemon juice
5 tbsp tahini
5 tbsp water
125ml (4floz) Greek-style yoghurt
salt, black pepper

Place chickpeas, garlic, cumin, tabasco, lemon juice, tahini,
water and yoghurt in a food processor or blender; pulse until
smooth. Add salt and pepper to taste. Cover and refrigerate
for 30 minutes to allow flavours to blend. Serve chilled.

THINK AHEAD
Make sauce up to 3 days in advance. Cover and refrigerate.

HONEY MISO SAUCE

MAKES 125ml (4floz)

4 tbsp miso (see page 159)
4 tbsp runny honey
1 tbsp creamy dijon mustard
2 tbsp grated fresh ginger
2 garlic cloves, crushed
1½ tbsp soy sauce
1½ tbsp cider vinegar

Whisk miso, honey, mustard, ginger, garlic, soy sauce and vinegar together until smooth. Cover and let stand for 30 minutes at room temperature to allow flavours to blend. Serve at room temperature.

THINK AHEAD
Make sauce up to 1 day in advance. Cover and store at room temperature.

CUCUMBER YOGHURT RAITA

MAKES 500ml (16floz)

1 unpeeled cucumber, seeded and grated
2 spring onions, finely chopped
1 garlic clove, crushed
½ tbsp grated fresh ginger
2 tbsp finely chopped fresh mint
3 tbsp lemon juice
375ml (13floz) Greek-style yoghurt
salt, black pepper
1 tsp cumin seeds, toasted

Combine cucumber, spring onion, garlic, ginger, mint, lemon juice and yoghurt. Add salt and pepper to taste. Cover and refrigerate for 30 minutes to allow flavours to blend. Sprinkle over cumin seeds. Serve chilled.

THINK AHEAD
Make raita up to 1 day in advance. Cover and refrigerate. Stir before serving.

CORIANDER COCONUT SAUCE

MAKES 500ml (16floz)

1 handful fresh coriander leaves
1 handful fresh mint leaves
4 garlic cloves, crushed
1 green chilli, seeded and chopped
1 avocado, halved and stoned
½ tsp ground cumin
1 tsp sugar
3 tbsp lime juice
200ml (7floz) coconut milk
salt, tabasco

Place coriander, mint, garlic, chilli, avocado, cumin, sugar, lime juice and coconut milk in a food processor or blender; pulse to a purée. Add salt and tabasco to taste. Cover and refrigerate for 30 minutes to allow flavours to blend. Serve chilled.

THINK AHEAD
Make sauce up to 1 day in advance. Cover and refrigerate. Stir before serving.

COOKS' NOTE
To prevent discoloration, store in a bowl with cling film, pressing directly on the sauce to prevent contact with air.

ROAST PEPPER AND BASIL SALSA

MAKES 250ml (8floz)

3 red peppers
2 garlic cloves, finely chopped
10 fresh basil leaves, torn
1 tbsp red wine vinegar
3 tbsp olive oil
salt, black pepper

Grill, peel and seed the peppers (see page 160). Cut into fine dice. Combine peppers, garlic, basil, vinegar and oil. Add salt and pepper to taste. Cover and let stand for 30 minutes at room temperature to allow flavours to blend.

THINK AHEAD
Make salsa up to 1 day in advance but add basil not more than 2 hours before serving. Cover and refrigerate. Bring back to room temperature and stir before serving.

MAKING FLAVOURED BUTTERS

Cut a piece of foil, approximately 25cm x 20cm (10in x 8in). Spread the butter in a block about 15cm (6in) long and 5cm (2in) thick in the middle of the foil. Roll up.

Twist the ends tightly to form an evenly shaped cylinder.

COOKS' NOTE

Flavoured butters are practical and easy. They can be made well in advance, frozen and sliced to order. Place a cold slice of flavoured butter on any food hot off the grill to create a simple, flavourful sauce with mininal effort.

CORIANDER CHILLI BUTTER

MAKES 15 SERVINGS

250g (8oz) unsalted butter, softened
1 handful fresh coriander, chopped
1 fresh red chilli, seeded and chopped

1 tbsp lime juice
2 tsp salt
1 tsp black pepper

Place ingredients in a food processor or blender; pulse until well blended. Wrap in foil (see opposite). Place in the freezer until hard, about 45 minutes. To serve, roll back foil and cut into 1cm (½in) slices. When slicing from frozen, warm the knife through under hot water first. After slicing, always tightly re-wrap the unused flavoured butter roll in the foil before returning to refrigerator or freezer.

THINK AHEAD
Make up to 6 weeks in advance and refrigerate. Alternatively, make up to 9 months in advance and place in freezer. To keep sliced butter chilled outdoors, float slices in a bowl of cold water and ice.

VARIATION
GARLIC PARSLEY BUTTER

MAKES 15 SERVINGS

Replace fresh coriander with the same amount of flat-leaf parsley. Replace lime juice with the same amount of lemon juice. Replace red chilli with 5 crushed garlic cloves.

BLUE CHEESE BUTTER

MAKES 15 SERVINGS

250g (8oz) unsalted butter, softened
125g (4oz) blue cheese

2 tsp black pepper

Place ingredients in a food processor or blender; pulse until well blended. Wrap in foil (see opposite). Place in the freezer until hard, about 45 minutes. To serve, roll back foil and cut into 1cm (½in) slices. When slicing from frozen, warm the knife through under hot water first. After slicing, always tightly re-wrap the unused flavoured butter roll in the foil before returning to refrigerator or freezer.

THINK AHEAD
Make up to 6 weeks in advance and refrigerate. Alternatively, make up to 9 months in advance and place in freezer. To keep sliced butter chilled outdoors, float slices in a bowl of cold water and ice.

VARIATION
BLACK OLIVE BUTTER

MAKES 15 SERVINGS

Replace blue cheese with 100g (3½oz) stoned black olives, chopped. Add 3 tbsp thyme leaves and 1 tsp salt. Reduce black pepper by 1 tsp.

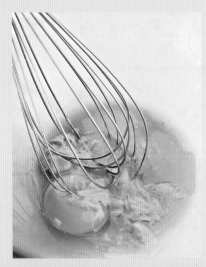

MAKING MAYONNAISE
Whisk the yolks until thick and creamy.

Add the oil in a steady stream.

MAYONNAISE

MAKES 300ml (10floz)

2 egg yolks
1 tsp creamy dijon mustard
1 tbsp red wine vinegar
½ tsp salt
pinch black pepper
150ml (5floz) sunflower oil
150ml (5floz) olive oil

Make sure that all the ingredients are at room temperature before you begin. Set a deep bowl on a cloth to prevent it from slipping as you whisk. Whisk the egg yolks, mustard, vinegar, salt and pepper together in a bowl until thick and creamy, 1 minute (see opposite).

Combine the oils in a jug. Whisk the oil into the egg yolk mixture a drop at a time until it thickens (see opposite). Add the remaining oil in a thin, steady stream, whisking constantly until thick and glossy. Whisk in any flavouring, if using, according to recipe variations opposite. Adjust seasoning, adding more mustard, vinegar, salt or pepper to taste.

THINK AHEAD
Make mayonnaise up to 3 days in advance. Cover and refrigerate. Return to room temperature before stirring to prevent the mayonnaise from separating.

COOKS' NOTE
If the ingredients are too cold or the oil is added too quickly, the mayonnaise may separate. Don't throw it away! Combine 1 tsp vinegar and 1 tsp creamy dijon mustard in a clean bowl. Whisk in the separated mayonnaise drop by drop until the mixture re-emulsifies.

USING READY MADE MAYONNAISE

Use ready made mayonnaise when in need of a time saving short-cut or if health concerns are an issue for you. Seek out a good quality whole egg brand of mayonnaise and freshen the flavour by whisking in creamy dijon mustard, sugar and red wine vinegar or lemon juice to taste.

USING A MACHINE

Follow recipe for mayonnaise. Place the egg yolks, mustard, vinegar, salt, pepper and sugar with 3 tbsp of the oil in a food processor or blender; process until blended, 10 seconds. While the machine is running, pour in the remaining oil in a thin, steady stream, until the mixture emulsifies and becomes thick and glossy. Pulse in any flavouring, if using. Adjust seasoning, adding more mustard, vinegar, salt or pepper to taste.

COOKS' NOTE
If using a food processor, depending on its capacity, you may need to stop the machine at intervals to scrape down the sides and over the base of the bowl with a spatula.

SAFETY WARNING ON RAW EGGS
Because of potential risk of salmonella, pregnant women, young children and anyone with a weakened immune system should avoid eating raw eggs. Make sure you use only the freshest (preferably organic) eggs, and if in doubt, substitute ready made mayonnaise (see above).

ROAST RED PEPPER AÏOLI

MAKES 300ml (10floz)
2 red peppers
1 recipe mayonnaise (see page 142)

Grill, peel and seed the peppers (see page 160). Place in food processor or blender; pulse until smooth. Whisk pepper purée into the mayonnaise.

ROAST GARLIC AÏOLI

MAKES 300ml (10floz)
1 head of garlic
I recipe mayonnaise (see page 142)

Slice off top of garlic, cutting through the cloves. Place cut-side up in oven tray. Drizzle over olive oil and sprinkle with salt and pepper. Preheat oven to 150°C (300°F) gas 2. Roast garlic head until completely soft, 1 hour. Leave to cool. Squeeze out cloves from papery skins. Mash until smooth. Whisk into mayonnaise.

CHILLI LIME MAYONNAISE

MAKES 300ml (10floz)
1 fresh green chilli, seeded and finely chopped
1 tbsp finely chopped fresh coriander
1 tbsp lime juice
1 recipe mayonnaise (see page 142)

Whisk chilli, coriander and lime juice into mayonnaise.

SALADS & SIDES

SLOW ROAST TOMATO SALAD

SERVES 4

6 tomatoes, halved
2 garlic cloves, finely sliced
1 tsp runny honey
1 tbsp balsamic vinegar
1 tbsp olive oil
salt, black pepper
1 tbsp chopped flat-leaf parsley
extra balsamic vinegar and
  olive oil to drizzle

Preheat oven to 150°C (300°F) gas 2.
Place tomato halves cut side up in an
oven tray. Place a garlic slice on top of
each half. Drizzle over honey, vinegar
and oil. Sprinkle with salt and pepper.
Roast until very soft and lightly charred,
1 hour. Sprinkle with parsley and drizzle
with oil and vinegar. Serve chilled or at
room temperature

THINK AHEAD
Roast tomatoes up to 1 day in advance. Cover and
refrigerate.

PARSLEY, MINT AND BULGUR SALAD WITH LEMON

SERVES 4

200g (7oz) bulgur wheat
200ml (7floz) boiling water
juice of 3 lemons
4 tbsp olive oil
2 tsp salt
1 tsp black pepper
1 tsp ground sumaq (optional)
4 medium tomatoes, seeded and diced
3 handfuls flat-leaf parsley leaves, roughly chopped
1 handful fresh mint leaves, torn

Place the bulgur wheat in a bowl. Pour over boiling water. Set aside until swollen
and tender, 30 minutes. Drain well, pressing to squeeze out excess water. Return to
the bowl. Pour over the lemon juice and oil. Add salt, pepper and sumaq (if using).
Add tomatoes, parsley and mint. Mix together until evenly combined. Serve chilled
or at room temperature.

THINK AHEAD
Prepare ingredients as directed up to 1 day in advance, but do not mix. Cover and refrigerate. Mix up to
1 hour before serving.

COOKS' NOTE
Sumaq is a dark burgundy coloured seed with a distinctive citrus tang often used in Lebanese, Iranian and
Syrian cuisine. You can buy it in powdered form from Middle-Eastern stores or by mail-order (see page 167). It
gives this refreshing, lemony salad an extra kick, but is not essential.

CREAMY POTATO SALAD WITH CELERY AND CHIVES

SERVES 4

750g (1½lb) new potatoes, cut
  into bite-size pieces
1 tsp creamy dijon mustard
1 tbsp red wine vinegar
2 tbsp olive oil
1 tsp salt
½ tsp black pepper
125g (4oz) cream cheese
150ml (5floz) Greek-style yoghurt
  or crème fraîche
2 celery sticks, finely diced
2½ tbsp finely chopped fresh chives
extra snipped fresh chives to garnish

Place potatoes in a large pan of cold
water. Bring to the boil. Gently simmer
until tender when pierced with the
tip of a knife, but still firm, 10-15
minutes. Drain.

In large bowl, mix mustard, vinegar, oil,
salt and pepper until smooth. Add hot
potatoes. Toss gently to coat each potato
piece. Set aside for 30 minutes to allow
flavours to combine.

Beat cream cheese and yoghurt or crème
fraîche until smooth. Stir in celery and
chives. Mix gently with potatoes to coat
evenly. Add salt and pepper to taste.
Refrigerate for at least 1 hour before
serving. Garnish with extra chives. Serve
chilled or at room temperature.

THINK AHEAD
Make salad up to 1 day in advance. Cover and
refrigerate.

COOKS' NOTE
If you can't find fresh chives, spring onions are also
excellent in this creamy, crunchy potato salad.

SESAME SOBA NOODLE SALAD

SERVES 4

2 tbsp sesame seeds
250g (8oz) soba noodles
3 tbsp shoyu (Japanese soy sauce)
1 tbsp sesame oil

Toast sesame seeds in a dry pan over a low heat until nutty and lightly coloured,
5 minutes. Set aside. Cook noodles in a large pan of boiling water until tender but
firm, 5 minutes. Drain and rinse in cold water to cool completely. Drain again.
Place in a bowl. Add toasted seeds, shoyu and oil. Mix gently to coat noodles.
Serve chilled or at room temperature

THINK AHEAD
Prepare salad up to 6 hours in advance. Cover and refrigerate.

COOKS' NOTE
Soba noodles are made from buckwheat flour. These greyish-brown Japanese noodles are available from
Asian stores, healthfood shops and most supermarkets. Alternatively, use Chinese egg noodles.

ORIENTAL NOODLE SALAD WITH CORIANDER AND LIME

SERVES 4

250g (8oz) rice vermicelli noodles
1 medium carrot, diagonally sliced,
  then cut into fine strips
¼ cucumber, diagonally sliced,
  then cut into fine strips
4 spring onions, diagonally sliced
2 fresh red chillies, seeded and
  finely sliced

2 tbsp chopped fresh coriander
  leaves
2 tbsp torn fresh mint leaves

FOR DRESSING
4 tbsp lime juice
4 tbsp fish sauce
2 tsp granulated sugar

Cook the noodles in a large pan of boiling water until tender but firm, 5 minutes.
Drain, then rinse in cold water to cool completely. Drain again. Roughly snip
noodles into smaller lengths with kitchen scissors.
For dressing, mix lime juice, fish sauce and sugar until sugar dissolves. Gently toss
noodles, carrot, cucumber, spring onion, chilli, coriander and mint with dressing
until well mixed. Serve chilled or at room temperature.

THINK AHEAD
Prepare noodles, salad ingredients and dressing up to 6 hours in advance. Store separately, covered and
refrigerated. Combine ingredients up to 1 hour before serving. Cover and refrigerate.

SMOKY BLACK BEAN SALAD

SERVES 4

**250g (8oz) dried black beans
  or 2 - 400g (14oz) tins black beans,
  drained and rinsed**

FOR DRESSING

2 garlic cloves, crushed
**1 chipotle chilli, seeded and finely
  chopped or 1 tsp chilli powder**
½ tsp ground cumin
½ tsp ground coriander
2 tsp salt
1 tsp black pepper
3 tbsp red wine vinegar
4 tbsp olive oil
1 recipe salsa fresca (see page 133)
6 tbsp crumbled feta cheese

If using dried beans, place in a large pan
with cold water to cover by 5cm (2in).
Bring to the boil. Boil hard for 10
minutes. Lower heat and simmer until
the beans are tender, 1-1½ hours. If
necessary, add hot water to keep beans
covered throughout the cooking time.
Drain thoroughly and set aside.

For dressing, combine garlic, chipotle or
chilli powder, cumin, coriander, salt,
pepper, vinegar and oil. If using dried
beans, pour dressing over hot cooked
beans. If using tinned beans, place
dressing in a small pan, bring to the boil
and pour hot dressing over rinsed tinned
beans. Mix gently to coat beans. Add
salt, pepper and more chilli powder to
taste. Set aside for 30 minutes to allow
flavours to combine.

Pour salsa fresca over beans. Sprinkle
with feta. Serve chilled or at room
temperature.

THINK AHEAD
Dress beans up to 1 day in advance. Cover and
refrigerate. Top with salsa and cheese up to 1 hour
before serving.

COOKS' NOTE
You can also use red kidney, black-eyed or pinto
beans for this recipe.

CREAMY CHIVE DRESSING

MAKES 125ml (4floz)

1 tbsp finely chopped fresh chives
2 tsp creamy dijon mustard
1 tsp granulated sugar
1 tbsp lemon juice
2 tbsp olive oil
8 tbsp Greek-style yoghurt or
  crème fraîche
salt, black pepper

Mix together chives, mustard, sugar, lemon juice, oil and yoghurt or crème fraîche until thick and smooth. Add salt and pepper to taste.

THINK AHEAD
Make dressing up to 1 day in advance. Cover and refrigerate.

HONEY MUSTARD DRESSING

MAKES 125ml (4floz)

1 garlic clove, crushed
1 tbsp runny honey
2 tbsp creamy dijon mustard
2 tbsp red wine vinegar
4 tbsp olive oil
2 tbsp crème fraîche or sour cream
salt, black pepper

Mix together garlic, honey, mustard, vinegar, oil and crème fraîche or sour cream until thick and smooth. Add salt and pepper to taste.

THINK AHEAD
Make dressing up to 1 day in advance. Cover and refrigerate.

BLUE CHEESE DRESSING

MAKES 125ml (4floz)

4 tbsp blue cheese, crumbled
1 tbsp finely chopped spring onions
2 tbsp red wine vinegar
2 tbsp sour cream
4 tbsp olive oil
salt, black pepper

Mix together blue cheese, spring onion, vinegar, sour cream and oil until combined. Add salt and pepper to taste.

THINK AHEAD
Make dressing up to 1 day in advance. Cover and refrigerate.

SPICY PITTA CHIPS

SERVES 4

4 pitta breads
6 tbsp olive oil
4 garlic cloves
½ tsp crushed chilli flakes
1 tsp dried oregano
1 tsp dried thyme
½ tsp salt
¼ tsp black pepper

Split pitta breads open into two. Combine oil, garlic, chilli, oregano, thyme, salt and pepper. Brush crumb sides of pitta halves with spicy oil. Grill or bake according to instructions below. Remove to a wire rack and leave to cool. Break into large pieces and serve.

OUTDOOR
Grill over medium-hot coals until golden brown, 1-2 minutes per side.

INDOOR
Preheat oven to 180°C (350°F) gas 4. Place oiled side up on baking sheet. Toast until golden brown, 5-8 minutes.

CRISPY GREEN LEAF SALAD

SERVES 4

1 iceberg lettuce heart, quartered
125ml (4floz) blue cheese, honey
  mustard or creamy chive dressing
  (see opposite)
salt, black pepper

Arrange the lettuce quarters on a platter and spoon over the dressing. Sprinkle with salt and pepper. Serve chilled or at room temperature.

COOKS' NOTE
Cos and Romaine lettuce hearts are also delicious with any of these dressings.

MAKING FOCACCIA DOUGH
Knead the dough until it is smooth, light and and elastic.

Cover the dough with a cloth and leave to rise until doubled in size.

FOCACCIA

SERVES 4 - 6

500g (1lb) strong white flour
2 tsp salt
325ml (11floz) tepid water
2 tsp dried yeast

2 tbsp olive oil
2 tsp fresh rosemary leaves
salt and pepper to sprinkle

Place the flour in a bowl. Make a well in the middle and sprinkle the salt around the edges. Pour the water into the well and sprinkle over the yeast. Leave for 5 minutes to allow the yeast to soften, then stir to dissolve. Add olive oil to the mixture.

Draw in the rest of the flour to make a rough, sticky dough. Turn out on to a lightly floured surface and knead for 10 minutes, until smooth, light and elastic (see opposite). Put back into the bowl, cover with a cloth and leave until doubled in size, about 1½ hours (see opposite).

Preheat the oven to 200°C (400°F) Gas 6. Deflate the dough by pressing down with the palm of your hand. Roll out into a flat round about 23cm (9in) across and place on an oiled baking sheet. Sprinkle with rosemary leaves, salt and pepper, or top according to the variations below. Cover with a cloth and leave until risen, about 30 minutes. Bake until bread is puffed and crisp on top, about 30 minutes. Cool on a wire rack. Serve warm, sprinkled with coarse salt and cut into wedges.

THINK AHEAD
Make and knead the dough and leave to rise in the refrigerator for 8-12 hours. Leave to stand at room temperature for half an hour before knocking back and shaping again. Rise again and bake according to the recipe. Alternatively, bake focaccia 1 day in advance and reheat in a hot oven for 15 minutes.

POTATO FOCACCIA WITH THYME

SERVES 4 - 6

1 recipe unbaked
  focaccia dough (see above)

FOR TOPPING
500g (1lb) baby potatoes
125g (4oz) gruyère cheese, grated
2 tsp fresh thyme leaves
4 tbsp crème fraîche

Prepare dough according to recipe above. Leave to rise through the second step. Preheat the oven to 200°C (400°F) gas 6. Cut potatoes into 0.5cm (¼in) slices. Bring a pan of salted water to the boil, add the potatoes, bring back to the boil and cook until the centres are just tender when pricked, about 5 minutes. Drain well and cool.
Shape dough according to the third step in the recipe above. Sprinkle half the cheese on top of the shaped dough. Arrange the potato slices over cheese. Scatter over remaining cheese. Sprinkle with thyme, salt and pepper. Dot potatoes with crème fraîche.
Bake until bread is puffed and topping is crisp, about 30 minutes.

ROAST ONION FOCACCIA WITH ROSEMARY

SERVES 4 - 6

1 recipe unbaked focaccia dough
  (see above)

FOR TOPPING
3 red onions, cut into wedges
1 tbsp olive oil
125g (4oz) gruyère cheese, grated
2 tsp chopped fresh rosemary leaves
salt, black pepper

Prepare dough according to recipe above. Leave to rise through the second step. Preheat the oven to 200°C (400°F) gas 6. Place onions in an oven tray. Drizzle with oil. Roast until soft and wilted, 30 minutes. Cool.
Shape dough according to the third step in the recipe above. Sprinkle half the cheese evenly on top of the shaped dough. Arrange onions over cheese. Scatter over remaining cheese. Sprinkle with rosemary, salt and pepper.
Bake until bread is puffed and topping is crisp, about 30 minutes.

THE MENUS

NUEVO TEX-MEX

A real crowd-pleaser: south of the border classics meet fresher, bolder flavours for great, gutsy food. Everyone will love this fun fiesta of wraps, chips, salsas and dips. Icy cold beers, please!

Creamy Avocado Salsa
(see page 132)
Store-bought tortilla chips
•
Spicy Lime Chicken Wings
(see page 101)
Chargrilled Quesadillas with
Spicy Coriander
(see page 128)
•
Spiced Beef Fajitas with Salsa
Fresca and Guacamole
(see page 38)
Smoky Black Bean Salad
(see page 151)
•
Premium brand chocolate ice-cream

DISTINCTLY MOORISH

Aromatic spices, fragrant herbs and refreshing citrus flavours make this Moroccan-inspired menu a delight for all the senses.

Honey Harissa Kofte
(see page 60)
Spiced Chickpea Sauce
(see page 137)
Spicy Pitta Chips
(see page 152)
•
Coriander Lamb Pitta Wraps
(see page 58)
Parsley, Mint and Bulgur Salad
with Lemon
(see page 147)
•
Grill Roast Sweet
Spiced Oranges
(see page 126)

VEGETARIAN FEAST

As the vegetables come hot off the grill, arrange them on large platters, spoon over the sauces and let everyone help themselves. You can make the focaccia and sauces a day ahead; refer to our THINK AHEAD notes.

Creamy Blue Cheese Sauce
(see page 133)
Spicy Pitta Chips
(see page 152)
•
Chargrilled Aubergine Slices
with Lemon Tahini Sauce
(see page 122)
Chargrilled Courgettes with
Roast Pepper and Basil Salsa
(see page 123)
Chargrilled New Potato Skewers
(see page 120)
Roast Onion Focaccia with
Rosemary
(see page 155)

BARBECUE ON THE BEACH

A beach is, of course, not essential. The backyard will do, but plenty of lemon wedges and paper napkins are a must. We suggest a well-chilled crisp white wine to accompany this celebration of seafood.

Clams in Coriander Chilli Butter
(see page 74)
Squid with Tomato Avocado Salsa
(see page 69)
•
Provençal Seafood Grillade with
Lemon Fennel Dressing and Roast
Garlic Aïoli
(see page 86)
A crusty baguette
•
Bowlful of summer berries

REAL FAST MENU FOR ENTERTAINING

High-flavour, low-input dishes for the time-challenged cook. You can make this menu a last-minute affair or use our THINK AHEAD notes if you prefer to plan in advance.

Honey Soy Chicken Wings
(see page 101)
Spicy Peanut Sauce
(see page 136)
•
Rosemary Peppered Pork Chops
(see page 44)
Chargrilled Tomatoes
(see page 120)
Crispy Green Leaf Salad with
Creamy Chive Dressing
(see page 152)
•
Chargrilled Nectarines
(see page 125)
Premium brand vanilla ice-cream

ISLAND BARBECUE

A totally tropical menu. Warm spices, hot chilli, savoury seasonings and a dash of dark rum will bring the sunny flavours of the Caribbean to your backyard.

Lemon Chilli Prawns
(see page 66)
Pineapple Lime Salsa
(see page 134)

•

Skewered Bajaan Chicken
(see page 96)
Chargrilled Squash with Jerked Honey Rum Glaze
(see page 123)
Chargrilled Corn on the Cob with Coriander Chilli butter
(see page 119)

•

Grill Roast Cinnamon Rum Bananas
(see page 126)
Premium brand vanilla ice-cream

ASIAN FUSION

Eastern traditions meet western trends in this simple, fresh and stylish menu bursting with vibrant flavours.

Spicy Masala Prawns
(see page 64)
Thai Spiced Chicken Wings
(see page 100)
Coriander Coconut Sauce
(see page 138)

•

Spiced Soy Duck
(see page 113)
Sesame Soba Noodle Salad
(see page 148)
Fresh Papaya Sambal
(see page 137)

•

Platter of chilled fresh tropical fruit

TUSCAN GRILL

A great menu if cooking for a crowd. You can bake the focaccia, prepare the lamb and grill the bruschetta and peppers a day ahead. A rich and rustic red wine perfectly complements this sensational sun-drenched menu.

Char-Roast Lemon Oregano Peppers on Bruschetta
(see page 129)

•

Lamb with Anchovy, Prosciutto and Parsley **(see page 54)**
Slow Roast Tomato Salad
(see page 147)
Potato Focaccia with Thyme
(see page 155)

•

Grill Roast Honey Orange Figs
(see page 126)

NOUVELLE GRILL

A thoroughly modern menu that combines global influences with contemporary inspirations.

Radish Tzatziki
(see page 135)
Spicy Pitta Chips
(see page 152)

•

Prawns with Tamarind Recado
(see page 67)
Pineapple Lime Salsa
(see page 134)

•

Spice-crusted Tuna with Thai Citrus Dressing
(see page 78)
Oriental Noodle Salad with Coriander and Lime
(see page 150)

•

Grill Roast Lemon Liqueur Strawberries
(see page 126)

NEW AMERICAN GRILL

A new look at patio cuisine! All the family favourites - drums, ribs and steaks with the influence of Asian and Latin flavours to replace the standard barbecue sauce. Our potato salad is as creamy as Mum's, but we make it lighter to suit today's tastes.

Honey Mustard Chicken Drumsticks
(see page 102)
Spiced Hoisin Ribs
(see page 48)

•

Chargrilled T-bone Steak with Chimi Churri Sauce
(see page 34)
Chargrilled Tomatoes
(see page 120)
Creamy Potato Salad with Celery and Chives
(see page 148)

•

Premium brand vanilla ice-cream

NOTES FROM THE COOKS ON INGREDIENTS

ACHIOTE SEASONING is a Mexican spice blend of ground annatto seeds, oregano, cumin, cinnamon, pepper and cloves. It is available powdered or as a paste from mail order or speciality stores (see page 167), or you can make your own (see page 23).

ANNATTO, also called achiote (see page 23), are the rusty red seeds of the annatto tree. Annatto is known as the saffron of Latin America, where it is used for its brick red colour and earthy flavour.

CAPERS are the pickled buds of the caper plant. Always drain well before using them.

CARAWAY SEEDS are aromatic seeds with a nutty, mildly anise flavour, widely used in Central European baking and cooking.

CARDAMOM is best used freshly ground as its fragrance diminishes with time. Crush lightly, open, discard the pods and grind the seeds (see page 161). If you are buying cardamom in the pod, choose green not brown cardamom for the recipes in this book.

CHILLI (see page 18) comes fresh, as powder or as flakes. There are over 200 different varieties of fresh chillies, varying in colour, size, shape and heat. When buying fresh chillies, make sure the stem is still on and that it is as fresh as possible; avoid any that have no stem. As a general rule, the smaller the chilli the hotter it is. Capsaicin, the substance in chillies responsible for their heat, can cause a very painful burning sensation if it comes into contact with the eyes or areas of sensitive skin. Make sure you wash your hands thoroughly after handling chillies. To reduce the level of heat, remove the seeds before using (see page 160).
Scotch bonnets are fresh, lantern-shaped chillies from the Caribbean with a fruity, citrus flavour and fiery heat. If you can't find them fresh, use Carribbean hot pepper sauce as an alternative and add drop by drop to taste.
Chilli powder is a hot seasoning of ground dried chillies, garlic, oregano, cumin and coriander. Pure chilli powders are ground from one variety of chilli without the addition of other spices and flavourings.
Ancho chilli powder is made from ground dried poblano chillies from the Americas. It is deep reddish brown in colour with a mildly pungent, rich, sun-dried flavour.
Kashmiri chilli powder is made from powdered Kashmiri chillies from India; it has a sweetish, pungent flavour without a burning heat.
Chipotles in Adobo are dried smoked jalapeño chillies, pickled and tinned in a piquant sauce made from chillies, herbs and vinegar. They are available by mail order or from speciality stores (see page 167).

CHILLI SAUCE is available in many different varieties. We use two types, and both can be found in large supermarkets or in Asian stores.
Chinese hot chilli sauce (see page 18) is made from chillies, salt and vinegar; use chilli sauce as an alternative.
Thai sweet chilli sauce (see page 19), flavoured with ginger and garlic as well as sugar, salt, vinegar and chillies, is often labelled "dipping sauce for chicken". If you can't find it, make your own. Combine 150ml (5floz) rice or cider vinegar with 4 tbsp granulated sugar in a small pan; stir to dissolve. Bring to the boil and simmer until syrupy, 5 minutes. Stir in ¼ tsp salt, 1 finely chopped garlic clove, ½ tsp grated ginger and 1 seeded and finely chopped red chilli. Cool before using. Cover and refrigerate for up to 1 week.

CHIPOTLES IN ADOBO (see chillies)

COCONUT MILK is available in tins from Asian stores and large super-markets. Shake well before opening.

FISH SAUCE (see page 19) is thin, salty, brown sauce made from fermented fish and used extensively in Southeast Asian cooking. It is available from large supermarkets, Asian stores or mail order (see page 167). We use Thai fish sauce called nam pla; use soy sauce as an alternative.

FIVE-SPICE POWDER is a Chinese spice blend of ground cloves, cinnamon, fennel, star anise and Szechwan pepper.

GINGER in its fresh form has a very different flavour from ground. Do not substitute ground ginger for fresh. Wrap and store fresh ginger in the refrigerator for up to 3 weeks. Cut off the skin with a sharp knife before grating (see page 160).
Pickled ginger (see page 20) is the Japanese condiment for sushi. It is easily recognised by its pink colour and is available in jars.

GREEK-STYLE YOGHURT is made from cow's or ewe's milk and is rich, creamy and flavourful. Use half sour cream and half whole milk yoghurt as an alternative.

HOISIN SAUCE (see page 20) is a slightly sweet, thick, dark brown sauce made from soy beans, garlic, and spices. It will keep indefinitely in a covered jar.

LEMON GRASS (see page 21) comes in long stalks and has a fragrant citrus flavour and aroma. Use only the tender inner stem as the outer leaves are tough. Lemon grass freezes very well, so you can buy it in quantity, freeze and use it as needed. As an alternative, use ½ tsp each of grated lime and lemon zest for 1 lemon grass stalk.

MIRIN is Japanese rice wine. It is sweeter than sake and used only for cooking. Use medium dry sherry as an alternative.

MISO (see page 20) is Japanese fermented soy bean paste. It is salty but highly nutritious. It is available in Asian stores, health food stores and large supermarkets. It comes in various colours and keeps indefinitely in the refrigerator.

MUSTARD comes in many forms, but we prefer to use smooth and creamy French Dijon. For a coarser texture, use grainy Dijon mustard.

PANCETTA is flavourful Italian streaky bacon. Store wrapped in the refrigerator for up to 3 weeks. Use streaky bacon as an alternative.

PEPPER should be freshly ground or cracked for maximum flavour. A good pepper grinder is an essential item for any cook who values flavour.

POMEGRANATE MOLASSES (see page 20) - also referred to as syrup or concentrate - is made by boiling down pomegranate juice to a thick, dark brown liquid with a distinctive sweet-sour flavour. It's a favourite flavouring across the Middle East, but especially in Iran, Syria and Lebanon. It is available in bottles from Middle-Eastern stores or by gourmet mail order (see page 167). Date molasses, which is readily found in healthfood stores, can be used as an alternative.

PRESERVED LEMONS are whole lemons pickled in salty lemon juice and used as a flavouring and condiment in Moroccan cooking.

PROSCIUTTO is Italian raw ham that has been seasoned, salt-cured and air-dried.

RICE NOODLES are Asian noodles made from rice flour. Use Chinese dried egg noodles as an alternative. Cook according to the package instructions.

SAKE is Japan's famous rice wine, widely used as a flavouring in Japanese sauces and marinades. Use dry sherry as an alternative.

SALT should always be sea salt, whether coarse or fine. The quality of salt matters. Different salts have different flavours and different degrees of saltiness. Salt draws out the moisture in meat, so we always season with it only after grilling.

SCOTCH BONNETS
(see chillies)

SESAME OIL (see page 20) is best when it is one of the Asian brands, and is extracted from toasted sesame seeds. Don't confuse this with the lighter sesame oil with a less intense flavour that is sold in healthfood stores.

SOBA NOODLES are very fine Japanese buckwheat noodles, available in Asian stores, healthfood stores and large supermarkets. Use Chinese dried egg noodles as an alternative. Cook according to the package instructions.

SOY SAUCE is a major seasoning in Asian cooking. It is available in a number of varieties, ranging in colour and flavour. We use light soy sauce when we wish to preserve the colour of the food but dark soy sauce has a richer flavour. **Japanese soy sauce**, called **shoyu**, is sweeter, lighter and less salty; use light soy sauce as an alternative.

SPICES should be bought whole and toasted and ground yourself, for the best flavour (see page 161). Even if you store them for a month or so, your home-ground spices will still be more flavourful than anything you buy ready ground from the supermarket.

TAHINI is a paste made from grinding roasted sesame seeds. It is sold in jars in large supermarkets, healthfood and Middle-Eastern stores. Shake well before using.

TAMARIND (see page 20) has a bright, sharp, tangy flavour. It is used mostly in Southeast Asian and Middle-Eastern cooking. It is available as jars of paste or concentrate or in blocks of sticky pulp. To use the pulp, dissolve in boiling water and sieve out the seeds: use ½ cup pulp to 1 cup water for a thick paste. It will keep in the refrigerator for up to 3 days, or you can freeze it in ice cube trays. Tamarind pulp and paste are available from Asian, Middle-Eastern and Hispanic stores, or by gourmet mail order (see page 167). Use freshly squeezed lime juice as an alternative.

VINEGAR comes in a variety of forms. **Red wine vinegar** (see page 21) and **white wine vinegar** have different flavours and levels of acidity and should not be used interchangeably. **Balsamic vinegar** (see page 21) is a widely available Italian vinegar; it is dark in colour with a sweet, pungent flavour. **Cider vinegar** is a mellow, fruity vinegar made from apple cider. **Rice vinegar** (see page 21) with its subtly sweet, mellow flavour, is used extensively in Japanese cooking. It is available in Asian stores and healthfood stores. Cider vinegar can be used as an alternative.

WASABI is a pungent green horseradish used in Japanese cuisine. It is available in dried powder form in tins and as a paste in tubes (see page 20). Use horseradish sauce as an alternative.

WHITE TRUFFLE OIL has a rich, earthy flavour and aroma and is delicious drizzled on pasta, risotto, vegetables and salads. It is available in small bottles from speciality or Italian stores, or from gourmet mail order sources (see page 167).

ESSENTIAL SKILLS

GRILLING AND PEELING PEPPERS
Grill peppers over a hot outdoor flame
or under a preheated indoor grill.
Turn as needed until blackened on all
sides, 10-15 minutes. Place in a plastic
bag or a bowl with a plate on top and
allow them to cool. Peel off the skin
using the tip of a small knife. Cut the
peppers into quarters and remove the
core. Scrape away seeds and discard.

REMOVING SEEDS FROM A CHILLI
Halve the chillies lengthwise with
a small, sharp knife. Scape out the
seeds and cut away the white ribs
from each half. Wash hands after
handling chillies.

CHOPPING AN ONION
Peel the onion, leaving the root end on.
Cut the onion in half and lay one half,
cut side down, on a chopping board.
With a sharp knife cut horizontally
towards the root end, and then
vertically. Be sure to cut just to the
root but not through it. Finally, cut
the onion crosswise into diced pieces.

PEELING A GARLIC CLOVE
Set the flat side of the knife on top
and strike it with your fist. This action
will loosen the skin, allowing it to peel
away easily by using your fingers.
Discard the skin.

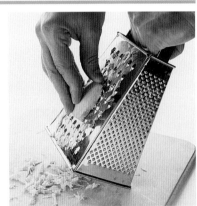

GRATING FRESH GINGER
Use a sharp knife or vegetable peeler
to cut away the skin from the ginger
root. Grate the ginger, making sure to
grate with the grain and not against it.

GRINDING WHOLE SPICES

Whole spices may be ground or cracked by hand in a mortar. Alternatively, to coarse grind or crack spices, place them in a plastic zip-lock bag and crush them with rolling pin or heavy saucepan. For large quantities, use a blender or food processor.

TOASTING SPICES

Place a dry cast iron pan over a medium-hot heat until hot, 2 minutes. Add the spices and toast, shaking the pan, until the spices are dark and aromatic, 5 minutes. Remove from pan and cool.

PEELING AND CHOPPING CITRUS

Cut a slice from the top and the bottom of the fruit. Cut away the rind, pith and skin, working from top to bottom and following the curve of the fruit. Slice the peeled fruit crosswise into 0.5cm (¼in) slices. Stack and chop the slices finely.

SEEDING TOMATOES

Cut the tomato in half crosswise. Gently squeeze each tomato half, pushing out the seeds with your fingertip.

MAKING CITRUS WEDGES

Cut the fruit in half lengthwise. Place cut side down on a board. Trim the stalk ends and discard. Cut each half across into 4 wedges.

INDEX

A

Achiote seasoning 158
  Recado rojo 23
acids, in flavouring 16
American menu: New American
  grill 157
ancho chilli powder 92, 158
anchovy, Butterflied leg of lamb
  with anchovy, prosciutto and
  parsley 54
annatto 21, 158
Asian fusion: menu 156
aubergines
  Char-roast aubergine with
    sesame and honey miso
    glaze 122
  Char-roast aubergine with
    spicy peanut sauce 122
  Chargrilled aubergine, goat's
    cheese and mint bruschetta
    129
  Chargrilled aubergine slices
    with lemon tahini sauce 122
avocados
  Avocado mango salsa 78, 136
  Chargrilled quesadillas with
    spicy coriander 128
  Citrus recado chicken breasts
    92
  Creamy avocado salsa 78, 96,
    101, 128, 132
  Squid with tomato avocado
    salsa 69

B

Baby squid stuffed with
  coriander and pickled ginger
  68
bacon, streaky: pancetta 159
baguette, Lemon oregano
  chicken baguette 95
balsamic vinegar 16, 21, 159
  Balsamic peppered pork
    chops 44
  Chargrilled balsamic red
    onions 118
  Crispy balsamic duck 111
bananas, Grill roast cinnamon
  rum bananas 126-7
basil, Roast pepper and basil
  salsa 77, 78, 123, 138-9
Beach barbecue: menu
  156

beans, Smoky black bean
  salad 151
beef 32-41
  fillet steak
    Chargrilled fillet steak
     with salsa verde 35
    Sesame soy skewered
     steaks 36-7
  minced chuck steak
    Best burger with blue
     cheese butter 41
    Coriander beef satays
     with honey tamarind
     glaze 40
    Hungarian spiced beef
     skewers with sour
     cream 39
  rump steak, Spiced beef
    fajitas with salsa fresca
    and guacamole 38
  sirloin steak, Chargrilled
    sirloin steak with garlic
    parsley butter 33
  T-bone steak, Chargrilled
    T-bone steak with chimi
    churri sauce 34
beer, Mussels in beer and
  garlic 74-5
Best burger with blue cheese
  butter 41
black beans, Smoky black
  bean salad 151
Black olive butter 140-1
  Leg of lamb steaks with
    black olive butter 55
Blue cheese butter 140-1
  Best burger with blue
    cheese butter 41
Blue cheese dressing 152
brandy, Grill roast sweet
  spiced oranges 126-7
breads
  Lemon oregano chicken
    baguette 95
  Red snapper tacos with
    chilli lime mayo 85
  see also bruschetta; focaccia;
    pitta breads; tortillas
bruschetta
  Char-roast lemon oregano
    peppers on bruschetta 129
  Chargrilled aubergine, goat's
    cheese and mint
    bruschetta 129

Spicy marinated squid on
  bruschetta 70
bulgur wheat, Parsley, mint and
  bulgur salad with lemon 147
burgers
  Best burger with blue cheese
    butter 41
  Herbed burgers 41
  Spicy burger 41
butterflied meat 54, 94, 96
  Butterflied leg of lamb with
    anchovy, prosciutto and
    parsley 54
  Butterflied leg of lamb
    persillade 56-7
  Leg of lamb steaks with black
    olive butter 55
butters, flavoured 140-1

C

Cajun seasoning 22
  Carolina honey glaze 22
capers 158
capsicum family *see* chillies;
  peppers
caraway seeds 158
cardamom 158
  Cardamom chicken tikka 108
Carolina honey glaze 22
celery, Creamy potato salad
  with celery and chives 148-9
Char-roast aubergine with
  sesame and honey miso glaze
  122
Char-roast aubergine with spicy
  peanut sauce 122
Char-roast lemon oregano
  peppers on bruschetta 129
Char-roast peppers 119
Char-roast rosemary onions 118
charcoal 7, 12
Chargrilled aubergine, goat's
  cheese and mint bruschetta
  129
Chargrilled aubergine slices
  with lemon tahini sauce 122
Chargrilled balsamic red onions
  118
Chargrilled corn on the cob
  with coriander chilli butter
  119
Chargrilled courgettes with
  roast pepper and basil salsa
  123

Chargrilled fillet steak with
  salsa verde 35
Chargrilled garlic potato slices
  120
Chargrilled lobster with garlic
  parsley butter 72-3
Chargrilled nectarines 125
Chargrilled new potato
  skewers 120-1
Chargrilled pineapple with
  jerked honey rum glaze 125
Chargrilled pineapple with
  sweet rum glaze 125
Chargrilled quesadillas with
  salsa fresca 128
Chargrilled quesadillas with
  spicy coriander 128
Chargrilled sardines 78-9
Chargrilled sea bass with
  fennel, lemon and olive oil
  80-1
Chargrilled sirloin steak with
  garlic parsley butter 33
Chargrilled squash with jerked
  honey rum glaze 123
Chargrilled swordfish with
  roast pepper and basil
  salsa 77
Chargrilled T-bone steak with
  chimi churri sauce 34
Chargrilled tomatoes 120
Chargrilled trout with garlic
  parsley butter 84
Charmoula 23, 96
  Charmoula lamb kofte 60
  Lemon charmoula squid
    70-1
  Moroccan spiced mackerel
    82-3
cheese
  blue cheese
    Best burger with blue
     cheese butter 41
    Blue cheese butter 140-1
    Blue cheese dressing 152
    Creamy blue cheese sauce
     106, 118, 133
  feta cheese, Chargrilled
    quesadillas with salsa
    fresca 128
  goat's cheese, Chargrilled
    aubergine, goat's cheese
    and mint bruschetta
    129

gruyère
Chargrilled quesadillas with salsa fresca **128**
Chargrilled quesadillas with spicy coriander **128**
Potato focaccia with thyme **154-5**
Roast onion focaccia with rosemary **154-5**
chicken 89-110, 114
grilling times 13
chicken breasts 92, 94
Chicken, prosciutto and sage skewers **96-7**
Citrus recado chicken breasts **92**
Ginger soy chicken breasts **93**
Herbed balsamic chicken breasts **93**
Lemon oregano chicken baguette **95**
Lemon yoghurt chicken wrap **98**
Skewered bajaan chicken **96**
Sweet chilli chicken **98-9**
Thai lime and coconut chicken **94**
chicken drumsticks 102
Honey mustard chicken drumsticks **102**
Lemon ginger chicken drumsticks with mango and mustard seed glaze **103**
Spicy tandoori chicken drumsticks **103**
Chicken legs stuffed with wild mushrooms **104-5**
chicken thighs
Cardamom chicken tikka **108**
Curried coconut chicken **106**
Ginger hoisin chicken skewers **107**
Tarragon mustard chicken skewers **106**
Teriyaki chicken **108-9**
chicken wings
Honey soy chicken wings **101**
Spicy lime chicken wings **101**
Thai-spiced chicken wings **100**
chickpeas, Spiced chickpea sauce 55, 60, 61, **137**
chilli flakes 17, 19
chilli powders 17, 19, 64, 158
chilli sauce 19, 158
Thai sweet chilli sauce 17, 19, 48, 158
chillies 17, 18-19, **158**

removing seeds 160
Chilli lime mayonnaise **143**
Red snapper tacos with chilli lime mayo **85**
Coriander chilli butter 41, 73, 74, 119, **140-1**
Chimi churri 83, **135**
Chargrilled T-bone steak with chimi churri sauce **34**
Chinese hot chilli sauce 19, 158
chipotles in adobo 19, 158
chives
Creamy chive dressing **152**
Creamy potato salad with celery and chives **148-9**
ciabatta
Char-roast lemon oregano peppers on bruschetta **129**
Chargrilled aubergine, goat's cheese and mint bruschetta **129**
Spicy marinated squid on bruschetta **70**
Cinnamon quail with pomegranate glaze **114**
citrus fruits 21
juices in flavouring 16
peeling and chopping; making wedges 161
see also lemons; limes; oranges
Citrus recado chicken breasts **92**
Clams in coriander chilli butter **74**
coconut milk 158
Coriander coconut sauce 93, **138**
Curried coconut chicken **106**
Spiced coconut lamb satays **59**
Thai lime and coconut chicken **94**
cooking times 8, 13
coriander
Baby squid stuffed with coriander and pickled ginger **68**
Chargrilled quesadillas with spicy coriander **128**
Chilli lime mayonnaise **143**
Coriander beef satays with honey tamarind glaze **40**
Coriander chilli butter 73, **140-1**

Chargrilled corn on the cob with coriander chilli butter **119**
Clams in coriander chilli butter **74**
Spicy burger **41**
Coriander coconut sauce 93, **138**
Ginger soy chicken breasts **93**
Coriander lamb pitta wrap **58**
Oriental noodle salad with coriander and lime 68, 106, **150**
courgettes, Chargrilled courgettes with roast pepper and basil salsa **123**
Creamy avocado salsa 78, **132**
Chargrilled quesadillas with salsa fresca **128**
Skewered bajaan chicken **96**
Spicy lime chicken wings **101**
Creamy blue cheese sauce 118, **133**
Tarragon mustard chicken skewers **106**
Creamy chive dressing **152**
Creamy potato salad with celery and chives **148-9**
Crispy balsamic duck **111**
Crispy green leaf salad 113, **152-3**
Cucumber yoghurt raita **138**
Cardamom chicken tikka **108**
Lamb tikka masala **59**
Curried coconut chicken **106**

D

Distinctly Moorish: menu 156
duck breasts 111
Crispy balsamic duck **111**
Duck with sweet orange glaze **113**
Spiced soy duck **112-13**

E

Eggs, raw: safety warning 142
equipment
grills 7, 8-9
for marinating 26-7
for measuring 7
tools 10-11, 104

F

Fajitas, Spiced beef fajitas with salsa fresca and guacamole **38**

fennel
Chargrilled sea bass with fennel, lemon and olive oil **80-1**
Provençal seafood grillade with lemon fennel dressing and roast garlic aïoli **86-7**
figs, Grill roast honey orange figs **126-7**
fire, heat control 12
fish 76-85
grilling times 13
see also seafood
fish sauce 17, 158
five-spice powder 158
Flame-roast lobster **73**
flatbreads
Coriander lamb pitta wrap **58**
Lemon yoghurt chicken wrap **98**
Spicy pitta chips **152**
flavoured butters **140-1**
flavours 14-28
principles 16
Focaccia **154-5**
Potato focaccia with thyme **154-5**
Roast onion focaccia with rosemary 111, **154-5**
Fresh papaya sambal 113, **137**
Thai lime and coconut chicken **94**
fruit on the grill 125-7

G

Garam masala 25
Curried coconut chicken **106**
Lamb tikka masala **59**
Spicy masala prawns **64-5**
garlic 16, 21
peeling 160
Garlic mustard pork skewers **48**
Garlic parsley butter **140-1**
Chargrilled lobster with garlic parsley butter **72-3**
Chargrilled sirloin steak with garlic parsley butter **33**
Chargrilled trout with garlic parsley butter **84**
Herbed burger **41**
Garlic sausages **50**

Roast garlic aïoli 73, 86, 95, 98, 102, 110, 119, **143**
  Skewered cumin lamb with garlic yoghurt sauce **61**
ginger, fresh 16, 21, 158
  grating 160
  Ginger hoisin chicken skewers **107**
  Ginger soy chicken breasts **93**
ginger, pickled 21, 158
  Baby squid stuffed with coriander and pickled ginger **68**
Grand Marnier, Grill roast lemon liqueur strawberries **126-7**
grey mullet
  Chargrilled sea bass with fennel, lemon and olive oil **80-1**
  Provençal seafood grillade with lemon fennel dressing **86-7**
Grill roast cinnamon rum bananas **126-7**
Grill roast honey orange figs **126-7**
Grill roast lemon liqueur strawberries **126-7**
Grill roast sweet spiced oranges **126-7**
grilling times 8, 13
grills 7, 8-9
  heat control 12
  preheating 7
grouper
  Chargrilled sea bass with fennel, lemon and olive oil **80-1**
  Red snapper tacos with chilli lime mayo **85**
guacamole, Spiced beef fajitas with salsa fresca and guacamole **38**

H
Halibut 76
  Chargrilled swordfish with roast pepper and basil salsa **77**
ham *see* prosciutto
heat control 12
Herbed balsamic chicken breasts **93**
Herbed burger **41**
Herbed salmon with tomato vinaigrette **81**

herbs, dried
  in flavouring 16
  herbes de Provence 21, 93
  Herbed balsamic chicken breasts **93**
herbs, fresh
  alternative to basting brush 104
  in flavouring 16
hoisin sauce 21, 158
  Ginger hoisin chicken skewers **107**
  Spiced hoisin ribs **48**
  Sweet soy glazed pork **46**
honey 16
  Carolina honey glaze **22**
  Chargrilled pineapple with sweet rum glaze **125**
  Coriander beef satays with honey tamarind glaze **40**
  Duck with sweet orange glaze **113**
  Grill roast honey orange figs **126-7**
  Honey harissa kofte **60**
  Honey miso sauce **138**
    Char-roast aubergine with sesame and honey miso glaze **122**
  Honey mustard chicken drumsticks **102**
  Honey mustard dressing 113, **152**
  Honey soy chicken wings **101**
  Jerked honey rum glaze 25, 123, 125
horseradish: wasabi 21, 159
Hungarian spiced beef skewers with sour cream **39**

I
Ingredients: notes 158-9
Island barbecue: menu 157

J
Jamaican jerk seasoning 24
jerk rub, Spicy 24, 96, 110
Jerked honey rum glaze 25
  Chargrilled pineapple with jerked honey rum glaze **125**
  Chargrilled squash with jerked honey rum glaze **123**

K
Kashmiri chilli powder 64, 158

L
Lager, Mussels in beer and garlic **74-5**
lamb 52-61
  boneless lamb
    Coriander lamb pitta wrap **58**
    Lamb tikka masala **59**
    Spiced coconut lamb satays **59**
  lamb chops, Rosemary lamb chops with mustard mint dressing **53**
  leg of lamb
    Butterflied leg of lamb with anchovy, prosciutto and parsley **54**
    Butterflied leg of lamb persillade **56-7**
    Leg of lamb steaks with black olive butter **55**
  minced lamb
    Charmoula lamb kofte **60**
    Honey harissa kofte **60**
  neck fillets, Skewered cumin lamb with garlic yoghurt sauce **61**
langoustines, Provençal seafood grillade with lemon fennel dressing **86-7**
lemon grass 16, 21, 158
lemon juice
  Char-roast lemon oregano peppers on bruschetta **129**
  Lemon chilli prawns **66**
  Lemon ginger chicken drumsticks with mango and mustard seed glaze **103**
  Lemon tahini sauce **132**
    Chargrilled aubergine, goat's cheese and mint bruschetta **129**
    Coriander lamb pitta wrap **58**
  Lemon yoghurt chicken wrap **98**
  Provençal seafood grillade with lemon fennel dressing and roast garlic aïoli **86-7**
lemons
  preserved 159
  Lemon charmoula squid **70-1**
  Lemon oregano chicken baguette **95**
  Lemon peppered poussin **110**

Provençal seafood grillade with lemon fennel dressing and roast garlic aïoli **86-7**
lettuce, Crispy green leaf salad 113, **152-3**
limes
  Chilli lime mayonnaise 85, **143**
  Oriental noodle salad with coriander and lime 68, 106, **150**
  Pineapple lime salsa 43, 67, **134**
  Spicy lime chicken wings **101**
  Spicy lime prawns **67**
lobster
  Chargrilled lobster with garlic parsley butter **72-3**
  Flame-roast lobster **73**

M
Mackerel 76
  Moroccan spiced mackerel **82-3**
mangoes
  Avocado mango salsa 78, 92, 128, **136**
  Lemon ginger chicken drumsticks with mango and mustard seed glaze **103**
marinating 26-7
mayonnaise **142**
  Chilli lime mayonnaise 85, **143**
  Roast garlic aïoli 73, 86, 95, 98, 102, 110, 119, **143**
  Roast red pepper aïoli 93, 96, **143**
measuring ingredients 7
meat on the grill 31-61, 89-110
  grilling times 13
menus 156-7
  Recado rojo 23
Mexican menu 156
Mexican spiced pork chops with pineapple lime salsa **43**
minced chuck steak
  Best burger with blue cheese butter **41**
  Coriander beef satays with honey tamarind glaze **40**
  Hungarian spiced beef skewers with sour cream **39**

minced lamb
Charmoula lamb kofte **60**
Honey harissa kofte **60**
minced pork
Garlic sausages **50**
Spicy sausages **50**
Toulouse sausages **50-1**
mint
Chargrilled aubergine, goat's cheese and mint bruschetta **129**
Parsley, mint and bulgur salad with lemon **147**
Rosemary lamb chops with mustard mint dressing **53**
mirin 158-9
miso 17, 21, 159
Honey miso sauce 122, **138**
molasses, pomegranate 16, 21, 159
monkfish, Chargrilled swordfish with roast pepper and basil salsa **77**
Moorish menu 156
Moroccan spiced mackerel **82-3**
mushrooms, wild 104
Chicken legs stuffed with wild mushrooms **104-5**
Mussels in beer and garlic **74-5**
mustard 159
Garlic mustard pork skewers **48**
Honey mustard dressing 113, **152**
Lemon ginger chicken drumsticks with mango and mustard seed glaze **103**
Rosemary lamb chops with mustard mint dressing **53**
Tarragon mustard chicken skewers **106**

N

Nam pla (Thai fish sauce) 19, 158
nectarines, Chargrilled nectarines **125**
New American grill: menu 157
noodles, rice 159
Oriental noodle salad with coriander and lime 106, **150**
noodles, soba 159
Sesame soba noodle salad 83, 113, **148**
Nouvelle grill: menu 157
Nuevo tex-mex: menu 156

O

Oils 16
olive oil 16, 21
Chargrilled sea bass with fennel, lemon and olive oil **80-1**
sesame oil 21, 159
white truffle oil 159
olives, Black olive butter 55, **140-1**
onions 16, 21
chopping 160
Char-roast rosemary onions **118**
Chargrilled balsamic red onions **118**
Roast onion focaccia with rosemary 111, **154-5**
oranges
Duck with sweet orange glaze **113**
Grill roast sweet spiced oranges **126-7**
oregano 16
Char-roast lemon oregano peppers on bruschetta **129**
Greek 21
Mexican 21
Oriental noodle salad with coriander and lime **150**
Curried coconut chicken **106**

P

Pancetta 159
papaya, Fresh papaya sambal 94, 113, **137**
paprika
Hungarian 21, 39
smoked 21, 48
parsley
Butterflied leg of lamb with anchovy, prosciutto and parsley **54**
Butterflied leg of lamb persillade **56-7**
Chimi churri 34, 83, **135**
Garlic parsley butter 33, 41, 73, 84, **140-1**
Parsley, mint and bulgur salad with lemon **147**
parties: real fast menu 156
peanut butter
Spicy peanut dip **136**
Spicy peanut sauce 47, 59, 101, 122, **136**

pepper; peppercorns 7, 16-17, 18, 19, 159
Balsamic peppered pork chops **44**
Rosemary peppered pork chops **44-5**
peppers
grilling and peeling **160**
Char-roast lemon oregano peppers on bruschetta **129**
Char-roast peppers **119**
Roast pepper and basil salsa 77, 78, 123, **138-9**
Roast red pepper aïoli 93, 96, **143**
pineapple
Chargrilled pineapple with jerked honey rum glaze **125**
Chargrilled pineapple with sweet rum glaze **125**
Pineapple lime salsa **134**
Mexican spiced pork chops with pineapple lime salsa **43**
Prawns with tamarind recado **67**
pitta breads
Coriander lamb pitta wrap **58**
Lemon yoghurt chicken wrap **98**
Spicy pitta chips **152**
pomegranate molasses 16, 21, 159
Cinnamon quail with pomegranate glaze **114**
pork 42-51
pork belly, streaky
Garlic sausages **50**
Spicy sausages **50**
Toulouse sausages **50-1**
pork chops
Balsamic peppered pork chops **44**
Mexican spiced pork chops with pineapple lime salsa **43**
Rosemary peppered pork chops **44-5**
pork fillet
Garlic mustard pork skewers **48**
Spicy pork satay **47**
Sweet soy glazed pork **46**
pork spareribs
Spiced hoisin ribs **48**
Thai sweet & sour ribs **48-9**
potatoes
Chargrilled garlic potato slices **120**

Chargrilled new potato skewers **120-1**
Creamy potato salad with celery and chives **148-9**
Potato focaccia with thyme **154-5**
poultry see chicken; duck; quail
poussin
Lemon peppered poussin 110, 114
Spicy jerk poussin 110, 114
prawns
Lemon chilli prawns **66**
Prawns with salsa fresca **64**
Prawns with tamarind recado **67**
Spicy lime prawns **67**
Spicy masala prawns **64-5**
Sweet sesame prawns **66**
preheating 7
prosciutto
Butterflied leg of lamb with anchovy, prosciutto and parsley **54**
Chicken, prosciutto and sage skewers **96-7**
Provençal seafood grillade with lemon fennel dressing and roast garlic aïoli **86-7**

Q

Quail
Cinnamon quail with pomegranate glaze **114**
Rosemary garlic quail **114**
quesadillas
Chargrilled quesadillas with salsa fresca **128**
Chargrilled quesadillas with spicy coriander **128**

R

Radish tzatziki 61, **135**
Honey harissa kofte **60**
Real fast menu for entertaining 156
Recado rojo **23**
recipes 7, 29-155
red mullet
Provençal seafood grillade with lemon fennel dressing **86-7**
Red snapper tacos with chilli lime mayo **85**

red snapper
  Chargrilled sea bass with
    fennel, lemon and olive oil
    80-1
  Red snapper tacos with chilli
    lime mayo **85**
red wine vinegar 21
rice noodles 159
  Oriental noodle salad with
    coriander and lime 150
rice vinegar 21, 159
Roast garlic aïoli 119, **143**
  Flame-roast lobster 73
  Honey mustard chicken
    drumsticks **102**
  Lemon oregano chicken
    baguette **95**
  Lemon peppered poussin 110
  Lemon yoghurt chicken wrap
    98
  Provençal seafood grillade
    with lemon fennel dressing
    and roast garlic aïoli **86-7**
Roast onion focaccia with
  rosemary 111, **154-5**
Roast pepper and basil salsa 78,
  138-9
  Chargrilled courgettes with
    roast pepper and basil salsa
    123
  Chargrilled swordfish with
    roast pepper and basil salsa
    77
Roast red pepper aïoli **143**
  Chicken, prosciutto and sage
    skewers **96-7**
  Herbed balsamic chicken
    breasts **93**
rosemary 16
  Char-roast rosemary onions
    118
  Roast onion focaccia with
    rosemary 111, **154-5**
  Rosemary garlic quail **114**
  Rosemary lamb chops with
    mustard mint dressing **53**
  Rosemary peppered pork
    chops **44-5**
rum
  Chargrilled pineapple with
    sweet rum glaze 125
  Grill roast cinnamon rum
    bananas 126-7
  Jerked honey rum glaze 25,
    123, 125

S

Safety precautions 9, 91, 142

sage, Chicken, prosciutto and
  sage skewers **96-7**
saké 159
salads & sides 144-55
salmon 76
  Chargrilled swordfish with
    roast pepper and basil
    salsa **77**
  Herbed salmon with tomato
    vinaigrette **81**
  Wasabi soy salmon with
    sesame soba noodles
    83
Salsa fresca 64, 78, **133**
  Chargrilled quesadillas with
    salsa fresca **128**
  Spiced beef fajitas with salsa
    fresca and guacamole **38**
Salsa verde **134**
  Butterflied leg of lamb with
    anchovy, prosciutto and
    parsley **54**
  Chargrilled sea bass with
    fennel, lemon and olive oil
    80-1
  Chargrilled fillet steak with
    salsa verde **35**
salsas and sauces 16, 131-39
salt 7, 16-17, 18-19, 159
sardines, Chargrilled sardines
  78-9
satays, Spiced coconut lamb
  satays **59**
sauces and salsas 16, 131-39
sausage casing 50
sausages
  Garlic sausages **50**
  Spicy sausages **50**
  Toulouse sausages **50-1**
Scotch bonnets 19, 158
sea bass
  Chargrilled sea bass with
    fennel, lemon and olive oil
    80-1
  Red snapper tacos with
    chilli lime mayo **85**
sea bream, Chargrilled sea
  bass with fennel, lemon
  and olive oil **80-1**
seafood 63-75, 86-7
  see also fish
sesame oil; sesame seeds 21,
  159
  Char-roast aubergine with
    sesame and honey miso
    glaze **122**
  Sesame soba noodle salad
    113, **148**

Wasabi soy salmon with
  sesame soba noodles **83**
Sesame soy skewered steaks
  36-7
Sweet sesame prawns **66**
shark, Chargrilled swordfish
  with roast pepper and basil
  salsa **77**
shoyu 159
  Baby squid stuffed with
    coriander and pickled
    ginger **68**
  Wasabi soy salmon with
    sesame soba noodles **83**
Skewered bajaan chicken **96**
Skewered cumin lamb with
  garlic yoghurt sauce **61**
Slow roast tomato salad 114,
  146-7
Smoky black bean salad **151**
snapper 76
soba noodles 159
  Sesame soba noodle salad 83,
    113, **148**
sour cream
  Chargrilled quesadillas with
    spicy coriander **128**
  Creamy avocado salsa 78, 96,
    101, 128, **132**
  Creamy blue cheese sauce
    106, 118, **133**
  Hungarian spiced beef
    skewers with sour cream **39**
soy sauce 17, 19, 159
  Honey soy chicken wings **101**
  Sesame soy skewered steaks
    36-7
  Spiced soy duck **112-13**
  Sweet soy glazed pork **46**
  see also shoyu
Spice-crusted tuna with Thai
  citrus dressing **78**
Spiced beef fajitas with salsa
  fresca and guacamole **38**
Spiced chickpea sauce 55, 61,
  137
  Charmoula lamb kofte **60**
  Spiced coconut lamb satays **59**
Spiced hoisin ribs **48**
Spiced soy duck **112-13**
spices 16, 20-1, 159
  grinding; toasting **161**
  see also chillies; pepper;
    salt etc
Spicy burger **41**
Spicy jerk poussin **110**
Spicy jerk rub 24, 96, 110
Spicy lime chicken wings **101**

Spicy lime prawns **67**
Spicy marinated squid on
  bruschetta **70**
Spicy masala prawns **64-5**
Spicy peanut dip **136**
Spicy peanut sauce **136**
  Char-roast aubergine
    with spicy peanut sauce
    122
  Honey soy chicken wings
    101
  Spiced coconut lamb satays
    59
Spicy pork satay **47**
Spicy pitta chips **152**
Spicy pork satay **47**
Spicy sausages **50**
Spicy tandoori chicken
  drumsticks **103**
Spicy tandoori mix **25**
Spicy tandoori chicken
  drumsticks **103**
squash, Chargrilled squash
  with jerked honey rum
  glaze **123**
squid
  Baby squid stuffed with
    coriander and pickled
    ginger **68**
  Lemon charmoula squid
    70-1
  Spicy marinated squid on
    bruschetta **70**
  Squid with tomato avocado
    salsa **69**
steak, *see under* beef
strawberries, Grill roast lemon
  liqueur strawberries **126-7**
sugar, dark brown, in
  flavouring 16
sumaq 147
  Parsley, mint and bulgur
    salad with lemon **147**
sweet & sour, Thai sweet &
  sour ribs **48-9**
Sweet chilli chicken **98-9**
sweet flavourings 16
sweet potatoes, Chargrilled
  garlic potato slices **120**
Sweet sesame prawns **66**
Sweet soy glazed pork **46**
sweetcorn, Chargrilled corn
  on the cob with coriander
  chilli butter **119**
swordfish 76
  Chargrilled swordfish with
    roast pepper and basil
    salsa **77**

T

Tabasco sauce 17, 19
tacos, Red snapper tacos with chilli lime mayo **85**
tahini 159
  Lemon tahini sauce 58, 122, **132**
tamarind 21, 159
tamarind paste 40
  Coriander beef satays with honey tamarind glaze **40**
  Prawns with tamarind recado **67**
tandoori
  Spicy tandoori chicken drumsticks **103**
  Spicy tandoori mix **25**, 103
Tarragon mustard chicken skewers **106**
tasting food 7
Teriyaki chicken **108-9**
Texan menu 156
Thai citrus dressing,
  Spice-crusted tuna with Thai citrus dressing **78**
Thai fish sauce 19, 158

Thai lime and coconut chicken **94**
Thai sweet & sour ribs **48-9**
Thai sweet chilli sauce 17, 19, 48, 158
Thai-spiced chicken wings **100**
thyme 16
  Black olive butter **140-1**
tikka
  Cardamom chicken tikka **108**
  Lamb tikka masala **59**
tomatoes
  seeding **161**
  Chargrilled tomatoes **120**
  Herbed salmon with tomato vinaigrette **81**
  Salsa fresca 38, 78, **133**
  Slow roast tomato salad 114, **146-7**
  Squid with tomato avocado salsa **69**
tortillas
  Chargrilled quesadillas with salsa fresca **128**
  Chargrilled quesadillas with spicy coriander **128**

Spiced beef fajitas with salsa fresca and guacamole **38**
Toulouse sausages **50-1**
trout, Chargrilled trout with garlic parsley butter **84**
truffle oil, white 159
tuna 76
  Provençal seafood grillade with lemon fennel dressing **86-7**
  Spice-crusted tuna with Thai citrus dressing **78**
Tuscan grill: menu 157

V

Vegetables on the grill 117-23, 128-9
vegetarian feast: menu 156
vinaigrette, Herbed salmon with tomato vinaigrette **81**
vinegars 16, 159
  balsamic vinegar 16, 21, 159
  Balsamic peppered pork chops **44**
  Chargrilled balsamic red onions **118**
  Crispy balsamic duck **111**

cider vinegar 159
red wine vinegar 21, 159
rice vinegar 21, 159
white wine vinegar 159

W

Wasabi 21, 159
  Wasabi soy salmon with sesame soba noodles **83**
white truffle oil 159

Y

Yoghurt 16
  Greek-style 158
  Cardamom chicken tikka **108**
  Cucumber yoghurt raita 59, **138**
  Lemon yoghurt chicken wrap **98**
  Radish tzatziki 60, 61, **135**
  Skewered cumin lamb with garlic yoghurt sauce **61**

Index compiled by Valerie Lewis Chandler

ABOUT THE AUTHORS

Eric Treuille has been passionate about food since he worked as a *mitron* (baby baker) in his uncle's boulangerie in south-west France. At the age of fourteen, he was apprenticed as a *charcutier* and went on to complete his culinary studies in Paris. He cooked professionally in Paris, London, and New York until work as a food stylist with Anne Willan and Le Cordon Bleu introduced him to the world of cookbooks. Currently director of the BOOKS FOR COOKS cooking school in Notting Hill, London, Eric is also the author of *Bread, Pasta, Canapés, The Organic Cookbook* and *Le Cordon Bleu's Complete Guide to Cooking Techniques*. He divides his time between the south of France, where he owns a vineyard, and London.
www.booksforcooks.com

Birgit Erath was born in the Black Forest region of Germany. Extensive travels across Africa, Asia, and the Americas—in particular the two years she spent cooking in the West Indies—expanded her culinary horizons and set her on a career as a spice trader. Her business rapidly burgeoned, from London's first market stall devoted to spices to a busy store bursting with over 1,800 culinary flavourings opposite BOOKS FOR COOKS in Notting Hill. She continues to travel in search of new sources for herbs and spices and new recipes for seasoning.
www.thespiceshop.co.uk

AUTHORS' ACKNOWLEDGEMENTS

We would like to thank:
Our three very special teams, who are, if you like, the rocks on which this enterprise is built.
The Books for Cooks team, but especially Victoria Blashford Snell, Jennifer Joyce, Kimiko Barber and Ursula Ferrigno. Their passion for food, both contemporary and traditional, remains a constant inspiration and we are eternally grateful for their willingness to share their discoveries with us.

The Covent Garden team, Stuart Jackman, Julia Pemberton Hellums, and Sally Somers for being just so fast, just so flexible, just so ready to do it! But perhaps this book really belongs to the studio team and especially Ian O'Leary, for being ready, willing and able to get out of the studio into the big outdoors. Things began pleasantly enough down on the farm in the late summer sunshine, but we had to work our way through a four seasons' worth of weather to arrive at that bitterly cold day in December in our back garden.
Photography in torrential rain was never so much fun.

HOW WE MAKE OUR BOOKS

In 1983, a tiny bookstore with a unique concept opened in London's Notting Hill. BOOKS FOR COOKS is a bookstore run by cooks for cooks, selling only cookbooks, teaching cooking classes, cooking from the books and serving up the results in a tiny restaurant among the bookshelves.

I work in the store, cook in the kitchen and teach in the school. It's true that I acquired my technical training as a professional chef, but, to my mind, my real culinary education began the day I crossed the threshold of BOOKS FOR COOKS. It's from my students and customers that I learn most about the way people live, cook and eat today, and it's this experience that informs the way we make our books. Real food for real life is our motto, and each title is specially devised to meet the needs of today's busy cooks.

I'm lucky enough to work in a team of dedicated food lovers. We research, test, photograph, write, design and edit our books from start to finish. All the ingredients are bought at ordinary shops and tested in a domestic kitchen. Our recipes are designed to be cooked at home. Oh yes, and it's all real food in the photographs!

You can write, phone, or e-mail us any time.

We'd love to hear from you.

Eric

BOOKS FOR COOKS
4 BLENHEIM CRESCENT
LONDON W11 1NN
TEL. 020-7221-1992

info@booksforcooks.com